THE POWERS OF HEAVEN AND EARTH

THE POWERS OF HEAVEN AND EARTH

NEW AND SELECTED POEMS

JOHN FREDERICK NIMS

Louisiana State University Press   Baton Rouge
2002

Manufactured in the United States of America
First printing
Cloth
11   10   09   08   07   06   05   04   03   02
5   4   3   2   1
Paper
11   10   09   08   07   06   05   04   03   02
5   4   3   2   1

Designer: Barbara Neely Bourgoyne
Typeface: Minion
Typesetter: Coghill Composition, Inc.
Printer and binder: Thomson-Shore, Inc.

ISBN 0-8071-2826-0 (cloth); ISBN 0-8071-2827-9 (pbk.)

Poems herein have been selected from *Five Young American Poets* (New Directions, 1944), *The Iron Pastoral* (William Sloane Associates, 1947), *A Fountain in Kentucky* (William Sloane Associates, 1950), *Knowledge of the Evening* (Rutgers, 1960), *Of Flesh and Bone* (Rutgers, 1967), *The Kiss: A Jambalaya* (Houghton Mifflin, 1976), *Zany in Denim* (University of Arkansas, 1990), and *The Six-Cornered Snowflake* (New Directions, 1990). Thanks go to the editors of the following publications, in which some of the new poems, or versions of them, first appeared: *American Scholar, Chronicles, Georgia Review, Harvard Review, Light, New Criterion, Nimrod, Sewanee Review*. "Freight" first appeared in *The Gettysburg Review*, volume II, number 3, and is reprinted here with the acknowledgment of the editors. "Love's Progress" and "Strange!" first appeared in *The Hudson Review*, volume XLVII, issue 3 (Autumn 1994). "Pascal on Ultrasound" and "The Seizure" first appeared in *The Kenyon Review*, new series, volume XVI, no. 1 (Winter 1994). "Cando Penso Que Te Fuches," "Die schöne Nacht," and "Now That You're Here" first appeared in *Poetry*.

Publication of this book has been supported by a grant from the National Endowment for the Arts in Washington, D.C., a federal agency.

For Bonnie

Now That You're Here

Now that you're here again, what's thirst or hunger?
What is there more than appetite can bring?
What's to expect from doorbells any longer,
And who's to come whose coming means a thing?

Why should I wait for mail, as in those barren
Days you were off in travel who knows where?
Why check the TV, local news or foreign?
You're *here*. So—rigorous logic!—nothing's there.

Why scan the papers, when the scrawny headlines,
Not brimmed with you, are pauperized of worth?
Why listen for the phone, its clamorous deadlines
Gone dead indeed from every town on earth?
All circuits in the world are down; here, here
Is the one cadence ravishing my ear.

They would not find me changed from him they knew—
Only more sure of all I thought was true.

—ROBERT FROST

CONTENTS

from Of Flesh and Bone, 1967

from The Kiss: A Jambalaya, 1982

from **Zany in Denim, 1990**

from **The Six-Cornered Snowflake, 1990**

NEW POEMS

The Mouse

This mouse that in my absence haunts the room,
Hunched in his sooty hood, his long palms livid—

When fiercely the lamp surprises him, caught midway
On the great acre of the desk-top, how he
Quivers, a bright-eyed panic with sharp ears.

Now comes the hunter's instinct, to fling books,
To whoop and poke and harass the little trophy.

But, one hand on the light-switch at the door,
I let him have the first move: flat and tightened
He palpitates a moment there, all nerves;
Then, trying to be invisible, nearly succeeding,
He races the cluttered alleys of the desk,
Skids in a dinky junkyard, inches long,
Of paper clips and golf tees, an old key ring.
Skirting the scholar's scribbled pack of cards
Über den ursprünglichen Text des König Lear,
He despairs of reversing his pretty descent
By trunk of desk-leg or electric liana,
Plops himself clumsy and squeaking to the floor
And under the wall-register scuds in a blur.

All in a moment. My hand leaves the switch;
I cross the room, stare at the desk, discover
What brought him his dark journey three floors up
Through gust and danger of hollow wall: the edge of
My amber artgum, nibbled fine, like coinage.

Take it, small earnest ghost.

            Myself, the giver,
Intrude here in the four walls of dimension,
And probably vex the economies of heaven.

The Powers of Heaven and Earth

Dolce e chiara è la notte . . .

I

One summer—I was four or so—we lived
In a musty-colored clapboard in the country;
Absentee Nooley owned it; it was "Nooley's."
The front door, from the parlor, opened on nothing:
No steps; we could hiphop down from it into the milkweed.
The barn was mostly skeletal; a ladder
Sagged to its sagging roof. Once, halfway up, I
Looked downward: dead leaves stirred, then came in focus
As a rattler coiled. I wrenched myself off sideways,
Streaked for the kitchen door, stepped on a nail
—A phrase of some foreboding then: it meant
Pre-antibiotic festering that lingered
In the sole of a foot like the Savior's in Mantegna.

In spite of the serpent there, it wasn't Eden.
The garden was radishes, rachitic carrots,
Some ruffles of lettuce, potato bugs under the leafage
Sartorial in their striping; these we picked and
Consigned to the fumes of kerosene in fruit-jars.
All of these, though—the snake, the gaudy insects,
The nail—I interpret by feelings that came later,
Remember as emblem only. Adumbrations.

II

Anyway, Nooley's. That was where I met
The powers of heaven and earth. My calcimined
Nook had a "little window where the sun
Came peeping in at morn," hinged horizontally
From the top; you'd push, then prop it wide with
kindling. Stretched tiptoe from my cot, I could just see out,
Which I did first thing most mornings. Over fields
Spectral with dew, off yonder but not far,
The railroad track ran glistening through cornfields.

4

The trains I'd do in crayon colors: Pullmans
In proper olive, royal blue, or cherry,
The oblong freights in purple, punkin, rust.

Then one day, one day only, the heavens opened.
I awoke, yawned, scrunched, uncurled, clutched for the window
And
    a *circus train*! In the yard almost! Just creeping.
Each car was—the word came later—psychedelic;
Outlandish calliope burled like a seashell, cages
Imperial in their panoply, every boxcar
Muraled with scenes of derring-do in jungles;
Each of them high baroque, a Renaissance altarpiece
—Bernini on wheels, I might have thought, years later,
As I thought of it once in a peacock-spread of fireworks
Over pomp of regattas on the Grand Canal.

So once in my life I woke to the apparitional,
To a jackpot strewn from the morning's cornucopia.

But the void when it rumbled by! the empty longing.

Did I go to the circus? Don't know. Just recall my
First view of the pomp and wonder of the world
Unfurling before me a moment, a *fragorío*
Like that of triumphant Rome poor Leopardi
Heard glorying over land and sea—then dwindling,
Her sinewy legions lost to dust and silence.

III

That was my morning memory. Now the night one,
And my mother's crooning tune to the *casta diva*.
A night of thunder and floodlit bursts of lightning,
Rain dinning the windows' timpani—kind of night she'd
Get up in a ghostly smock, her lavish curls

Afloat on her shoulder, wander and unfasten
The fronds of palm festooning her holy pictures,
Palms blessed at the altar, Sunday before Easter,
In memory of those the Lord on His donkey scuffed through.
Ancestral voices led her? It must have been something
From cabin thatch and the banshee airs of Eire.
She'd light the tips of the fronds in a chimney-lamp's
Blue flame and walk the shuddering house, her fingers
Flicking the myrrh of ash from leaf ends, till
It floated in flakes toward rag-rug and linoleum,
To save the house from lightning. As it did.
That it didn't burn down the house was another miracle.
Sometimes, to back up ash, she'd sprinkle water
Also blessed in the church. That special night
The thunder—in awe of her leafy hands?—had lessened
To a cool and pitchdark stillness. Then she took me
To a window, brushed the curtains back, and

there!

From between the jagged horror of two clouds
Such a flood of moonlight as I've not seen since,
All the more glamorous for the blackness round it:
The full moon, mottled with its scarps and craters,
Afloat magnetic there, a globe so luminous
The luster reflected in my mother's eyes.
Then she breathed something eerie, breathed a breathless
Spell in my ear: to think what heaven must be
If the merest country moon could pulsate such
Profusion of treasure! Did she mean, let's move
From Nooley's into the moon's hallucination?
Enough of the bugs and rattlers, rusty nails?
Whatever she meant, some meaning haunts me yet
—Beglamored young, is one ever at home in the world?

IV

I discovered the same moon later in Leopardi.
Distilling the honey of sunlight to its candor,

It rose unclouded through his moody vapors,
Bringing no comfort, none: no mothering spell
At cradle time left treasure for him. Treasure
Found is a longing lost; he kept his longing.
Still further back, through blinded vision Homer
Rejoiced in a windless moon. So all goes back
Past pyramid, cave painting, fossil footprint,
Back to deep time. The crust of the earth remembers
The carrousel of its animals in fracture,
Silurian wrack, Devonian wrack, the tar-pits,
Specters in carbon, amber; stranded hulls of
Iguanodons in the ginkgoes; bones embossed
Like the broken spokes of circus wheels; collected,
Some, in our cool museums;
                          some, gone deeper
Than even the moon can touch, for all her fingering.

Julianne-julienne

Julianne of Norwich, julienne of leeks,
Is that our range of options here below?
To haunt the cloud where pure Enigma speaks
Words so occult they leave the night aglow?
Or to *bonne-bouche* it? Napery! Cuisine!
Diamonds on warm fingers by our own
Languid on stemware, tilted wine between
Blossomy kisses, and then—then!—fullblown

Rumplings of bedded pleasure. How compare
Norwich and leeks? Soul, body? Yet the two
In intimacy mingle. Though somewhat spare
In others, their very plenitude's in you,
My Julianne-julienne. Your body's droll
Gala mélange! What setting for a soul!

Pascal on Ultrasound

"Just midway on the gurney of . . ." a dismal
Quip as they wheel me through fluorescent gloom,
Chill sheet to keep the chill off, down abysmal
Hallways of anesthesia to a room
Where vestured tall attendants, on TV
Consoles, enhance my heart with ultrasound:
Show it as fields of light; a galaxy
Grand as our own, it scintillates around,

Whirl within whirl complying, as entranced,
In systole, diastole, all parts
Dilating, cozying back—they danced! they danced!

Less awesome than your love though, still my heart's
Single prime mover. *Ces espaces . . . m'effraient?*
Not any more. I've been there. Know the way.

Celebrating a Birthday

The cannonballs, pintsize, now yoked together
On rods of brass—my veteran dumbbells—grow
Unwieldier year by year. I'm wondering whether
Burdened with rancors of their long ago?
Contagion of age is everywhere about me,
Quantum decay distorting time and space.
Why do the miles stretch wearier? Clocks, without me,
Elbow their way ahead in trendy chase?

Earth every day is clumsier. Stairs are stumbly;
Keys slip from fingers; floors are down too far.
Games show their age: balls bobble, thumbs are fumbly.
Mallets? They've turned flamingos—there you are!
Worse: mirrors once full-bodied, rose and gold,
Show withering apparitions. Old! They're old!

Love's Progress

I

One place: a grottoed recess in Liguria
Carved out of rockface by the restless sea;
An old inn there, a chapel of the Doria,
No entry but by boat: that summer, we
Dallied with lunch and wine and with each other,
Drunk with the sun and silliness as well,
Then—towel and swimsuit packed—in freshening weather
The boat's too cozy cockpit sealed the spell:

Much snuggling up, much kissing, smothered laughter
Curtained in windy valence of her hair,
Or so we thought, who, unaware till after,
Were studied by some dozen people there.
One bluff old salt, eyes twinkly, shrugged, "Should one
Practice these moonlight mysteries in the sun?"

II

So I learned loonier ways, rhymed "dune light . . . June light . . ."
Only, some weeks gone by, to dirge it so:
"Seeing our love, the affair of mist and moonlight,
Is water under a bridge burned long ago . . ."
I drawl it now; we laugh and lean together;
You wonder "Who she was?" No, I'll not say,
Except, it makes no difference if or whether.
"Love" was a windy labial till today.

Now love means *you*. *You/love*—the two synonymous.
Signposts all signal *you*, and that's my way.
Memory's awash in *you*; you've grown eponymous:
Places we've been become you. If, I say,
Each land we travel were renamed as *You*,
That name were truer than all maps are true.

The Opera

Callas. La Scala. *Tosca.* '53.
Strange, I remember only I was there.
Now the recordings haunt me: poignancy
Of "Vissi d'arte" can lacerate the air
When listening by myself. You were beside me
That evening in Milan. Were just *beside*?
No happier preposition?—Donne could guide me—
When touches, alert and thermal, first confide?

Recall that emperor, "Stupor Mundi"?—meaning
The World's Amazement. Meaning stupor too.
Glory can blind, as once it did by screening
Sets, theater, and diva. Close to you
Leaning, I dazzled in the sidewise light
Till love's halation became second sight.

The Silence

All night with others, with the rapturous few,
There have been times indeed, there have been times!
Times that ran out with everyone but you,
Leaving as memory the poor softshoe rhymes
That hush the names. Such names, though, stay with me
As in love's aftersleep where, grave and slow,
Breath learns dimension of the undulant sea.

And someone murmurs, out of long ago,
"Just now, astir from dreams, I heard your breathing,
And thought it ocean underneath this wharf . . ."

It was no dreme. You've seen a groundswell seething
Almost to maelstrom, with no sound of surf,
Or nearly none?
                        Seen how fad's blabbing book
Is far less passionate than one silent look?

Love and Other Wonders

I

You've noticed how the Mozart "Benedictus"
And Verdi's "Bevi! Bevi!" sound the same?
Same luring cadence in the devil's rictus
And heaven invoking the most holy name?
What do we make of this? Madonna, Sodom
So close, as Russian novels say? Here's grist
For any mill! As right needs left, top bottom,
Life feeds on contrariety to exist?

Days blithe and dire. But, by themselves, could either
Project in throbbing color grief or bliss?
Play feelingly its role without the other?
I'm with bewildered Viola in this:
"O Time, thou must untangle this, not I."
Time has no answer, though we try and try.

II

Time thunders on, all tunnel vision, glassy
Focus set dead ahead. But lazy Space,
Strewn at loose ends, eye vague, eructions gassy,
Shuffles cartoons by Euclid, moony face
Gaping on nests of nothingness we clutter
With urban sprawl and theory of stars.
Space has no answer but some astral mutter
Like the toy lightning in the Leyden jars.

The heart, though, long suspected to have reasons
The reason knows not of, might hint a way.
True, it keeps microtime, but flouts the seasons:
May in December, in December May.
Has no before or since, under, above.
Out of this world, the heart is. Call it love.

III

Love thrives on confrontation. Young, it doodles
Valentines, hearts—but arrows soon enough.
Would rather ride on tigers than walk poodles.
Its *Sic et Non* approves: the going's rough.
Love's one on one; for all our cant and blather
It does what others won't, or if they would
We shun the advances—often would die rather.
Suppose her course ran smooth, all options good,

No death impending—then what price fidelity?
Such plethora of flesh beneath the moon!
A year for Scarlett, and then one for Melanie,
Iseult one April, Juliet one June.
That's heaven? Or maybe hell? Souls pupa-size
A-flitting, from lip to lip, through simpering skies.

Till News of You

Wormholes in time. Hulls, hollows, hours and days
More cratered with vacuities than the moon;
Lassitude, languorings at dawn, malaise
Bogged in lacunas of the afternoon.
Longueurs of tile and porcelain; carious teeth,
The brushing, fussing, and next night again;
Boredom in airports, a lone beer beneath
The moon-face clock evasive about *when*.

Routes meant eroded ruts—till news of you
Brimmed every hollow with a glittering tide:
Sun on the spray reflecting rainbows through
Love's musty cottage, long unoccupied
—But now alive with light, shapes on the wall
Dancing like masquers at a gala ball.

A Memory of Places

Where the mad ocean breaks its teeth on stone
And exiled royalty has crept for haven,
We came to meet, and met, and were alone.
Love in Lisboa! Call it dove and raven.
Galicia next: like robins in the rain,
Chirp-chirping, the wagon wheels would creak us toward
Where crows in the Roman theater in Spain
Spoke in pure Poe their one bituminous word.

Estremadura and the bitter end.
But not the end; the end was Finisterre
And the mad gulls like gamecocks in the wind.

From decks at midnight, in the surf off there
Who'd strew your smouldering letters in the bay?
What whitecaps frothed as if to boil away?

Time's Arrow

I

The seaside lollings of our youth! One summer,
Gold as that sunflecked bevy in the dunes,
I read, between my viewings, most of Homer.
Easy as surf the lines rolled. But their tunes
Elude me now. The dactyls cramp. Old-Spanish
Lapses, the Cid's *deliço* dies away.
Galician rains, their *cómo chove,* vanish,
With Ariane, *de quel amour blessée.*

Sometimes I turn there yet; the works are shaling
Like castles once I knew, Sarzana where
Perché non spero set the copse a-wailing . . .
Texts, memories fail: they're *tabula rasa,* bare
And bleaching.
                          Love, illuminate me, scroll
With your calligraphy a decrepit soul.

II

That soul unburdened of the world's detritus
Would be like vellum for your *gesta,* gold
And cramoisi and vert—quaint terms invite us
Away from the day's devotions, "bought" and "sold,"
Though "bought and sold" befits the spend-or-save men,
Their greenbacks dated, numbered—look and see.
What's so ephemeral as the day is? Cavemen
Lived for it only, and lived meagerly.

"Love's not time's fool." Addendum: you're not either.
You're in the primal quantum world, where time
Runs both ways indistinguishably. Whether
Future or past, no telling. All's at prime.
You're time-invariant, love. And yet somehow
Splendidly bedded in the here and now.

Worth in the World

Worth in the world, what is it? Strand of leaves
Strung in the hair, play-acting old Apollo?
Or a mike-in-fist politico who achieves
Such thunder as resounds from any hollow?

A neon name curvaceous on façades
Where chink and jingle of coin are offering *Sanctus*?
Or flesh turned bronze or marble, above quads,
Bird-streaked, graffiti-twitted?

                       Such glories ranked us
With those presumptuous fame calls *Men of Worth*?
As if polls knew the valid from the vain!
When I sit mulling what avails on earth
Your love at once claims eminent domain,
Its world of worth! I've some too, in the end,
My worth in being your unworthiest friend.

The Seizure
Bernini in Winter

Snowfall at Christmas: windows here below
Gala with three-ring glories from above,
Their merry-go-rounds and ferris-wheels of snow
—Such, I whirl off on vertigoes of love:
Breath caught, lip bitten, and wit dispossessed,
Joy like angina closing on the heart.
A monstrous love! How hurl me to your breast
Or reach you even? With hand or any part?

How quench a worse-than-blood-does ravening lust?
By strewing in town the promos of your praise?
Hunched haggard in desert caves? With sermon's dust
In rack of pews choked upon holy days?
Or rapt, in lassitude, no thought but you,
Endure the seizure as loved women do?

Rilke Surmised

God knows I never loved any, no, not her
Whose least Dishevel at Night rocked the Blood's Rhythm,
Without seeing Sun in that wild Weather's Blur,
The One Ray split and crazied in that Prism.
God knows I dreamed, as Lips touch (dizzying Surge!),
Drowned Kings and Queens, lost Wealth, such dubious Freighting
As Michelangelo's "Caro . . . sonno" Dirge,
"Exaudi" of Mozart to high Heaven's Grating.

Everything (I learned this in Sobs and Kisses)
Is lifted from Nothing at all, to Nothing goes,
Unless the Revealing Voice, whose Burden this is,
—Our *Jubel und Ruhm!*—to Canticle transpose
All this! all this! Though some hail other Truth,
I sailed by this one in stark Weather of Youth.

Strange!

I'd have you known! It puzzles me forever
To hear, day in, day out, the words men use,
But never a single word about you, never.
Strange!—in your every gesture, worlds of news.
On busses people talk. On curbs I hear them;
In parks I listen, barbershop and bar.
In banks they murmur, and I sidle near them;
But none allude to you there. None so far.

I read books too, and turn the pages, spying:
You must be there, one beautiful as you!
But never, not by name. No planes are flying
Your name in lacy trailers past the blue
Marquees of heaven. No trumpets cry your fame.

Strange!—how no constellations spell your name!

Explicating "The Necromancers"

Flushed and in heat my verses all that summer
When love was riotous in the blood. One day
Our rented bikes had brought us, as so often,
From separate villas on the mountainous bay

To our sainte-chapelle ("St. Hideaway's"): sand and seagrass
Niched in the gothic rock, which interplay
Of wave and sun threw stained-glass aureoles over,
As seabirds choired. Gilt bodies snug, we lay,

Fingers enlacing. That day I came early,
Lay facedown waiting, heard her trail along
To ease in, close beside me, warm palm pillared
On my bare shoulder. "Wrong," she breathed, "it's wrong,

Meetings we hide from two who really love us,
Who, if they knew—"
                              Stark *if*!
                                        An autumn chill
From blackening clouds set bleaker blood a-stumble.
Some tears. Ink even more. For soon I'd quill

—*Quill!* No, more glib a tool. I'd ballpoint rather
"The Necromancers" with its sidling pun.
Swanky iambics strutting front in costume
To resonate their role. Such verses run

As: Tally the take in that affair with glory.
        How I lay gaudy on the blazoning shore,
        Face burrowing in a bed of fern, blood stirring
        Gamy as wines remembering summer stir.

        Off grottoes hung with corks and cordage bobbling
        By halcyons where the lascar and light o' love
        Lay fecund in feluccas, long we'd dawdle
        —Who cared that a plague of angels buzzed above?

No vein of all this flesh but leapt with memory,
With every sense in tremolo—rapt quintet!
Like noon on the bay a-blaze, or day's two-timing
Gilt-washed contrarious ikons, rise and set.

Deep comas of the sun! My drowsing shoulder
Ached for the sweetness pillared on her palm.
Ear to the ground heard—*shush!*—heard tambour of sandals,
Allegro of denim swirled. Ah, there's the psalm

Preluding our chapel rites! I felt her settle
In and alongside, warmth to warmth. A song
Thrilled in my muffled brow, "It's sun! It's honey!
That rush in the blood!" Her purred demurral, "Wrong . . ."

Long hair swung side to side, in sad negation,
"Wrong . . . !"
                    So admonishing autumn took the shore,
Where two had mimed, palms conjuring, devotions
The sea-crows now asperse, and neume no more.

The wheel that fractured light had come full circle.
Leaned with the poky spoke dust deepens on.
Ours sang and singing died. But all one summer
Who knew for sure that wonder from the sun?

Of all who grieved *tot milia formosarum*
I rate the least (decorum bids me say),
And yet know something of a splintered glory
Whose edge ran red, in dream at least: such play

Of *ill* offsetting *well*—off-rhyme, off-reason.
(Off guard, our ancient gods, that ripe July.)
A base clef darkening, while our *ooh*'s and croodles
Soured, with their tuneful nuisance, sea and sky.

The Only Text

The flesh, its fine calligraphy on bone!
The serifs, curls, and flourishes—her own!—
Spell *Warmth, Wit* . . . wistful tenderings . . .

                                                    "Enough!
Bodies spell *Mortal*! And the rest is—guff!"

Old mouldy *Mortal*! No, the live words arc
From living script to constellate the dark.
To puzzle out their mythologies above,
She taught me spelling as she taught me love.

Impervious

He strides in burly armor; not a chink
Where spear can pierce steel plate or rivet's link.
Fluted the flank, Milan her proudest ware,
Crested and chesty.
                    "And his name?"
                                    The pair
Of dragons, bat-winged on his helmet, brace
In claws of bronze an escutcheon: name and race.
"Himself! I might have known!"
                                The impervious sir
No pang can shake, no venturing lover stir.
Crustacean more than man: Sir Ego, he
Of Castle Pride, of stirps Stupidity.

Timepiece

Si quaeras, nescio . . .

The Past: that hungry gorge that swallows all.
We dance on the edge, pose, pirouette, and—

fall.

The Future: those gaudy dreams we preen us on,
Gone—*poof!*—in the scathing honesties of dawn.

Between them, a meager *Now,* its mien in doubt,
The mini-moment life's aglow,

then out.

"Path of Life"—cheesy oleo!

Path!

This shrill

Highwire above Niagara, set a-thrill
Beneath our feet, where—

Fanfares sound.

And so

. . . Left . . . right . . . above the abyss.

Don't look below.

The Day Our Dog Died

Grim six-foot Death, His Majesty in Black,
Stopped by; scooped up our pup; won't hand her back.
Stood. Stared at us—you, me. Then nodded twice.
Left, with his great cape flicking us. Like ice.

Love's Bittersweet

Shoulder so snowy, yet so cold? I'd grieve—
"Snowy *yet* cold? *Yet* yet! You've taken leave—"
Of my senses, yes.
           Sense!
               Boor that bars the door on
Sweet Aphrodite, lip luring, accent foreign
—So shy, so wild—in her true tongue, oxymoron.

The Beautiful Atheist

Canzonetta sull' aria

In bed, as the feathers flew, push came to shove:

"The Beard!" she teased. "His Regalia'd Babe! Their Dove
Yoohooing in tongues! Your three-ring show above!"

       Your klutzy puppetry, love. I've notions of
       A something other—

              "You've *notions*! Fact's the glove
I'd fling in their face, your notions! Dear, you'd shove
Fact under some mythy rug, no?"

           Then the Dove
      Descending in flame—?

            "*I*'m flame. In my eyes look, love—"

Dark pools, so aflow with light! From the moon above—

"Beard, Babe, Bird lost in its glow?"

            —where hand in glove
      Joy leads us, Lord of the Dance, through fullness of
      The effulgence

        spectral

          in our nights of love.

Scientist's Morning Prayer

While kids, with their blocks, build things of A B C,
We build, with our quarks and leptons, theory.
Help us pile π, our mc^2, our whatsies
Into Grand Unified Theories (our GUTsies),
As You, Lord, help when pudgy fingers prop
Two blocks on three and—*ooh, lookee!*—one on top.

Porno People

O love, that moves the sun and the other stars,
These too you move to their hooded avatars.
Your luminous noon they flee, to hug your shade,
Haunting dim ferneries or the louche arcade.
Squirmy in church, they know not what they do,
Going down, though not on knees, to worship you.

Così

In love with Dorabella all that autumn,
In love with Fiordiligi come the spring
—"Oh no you weren't!" fact bristles. Daft about 'em
Is what I was. Delicious names to sing.
Bald fact now, that's your fuddyduddy daddy
Of one idea: to have a world just so.
He never had a gaudier notion, had he?
Round every "Yes" his clump of cactus, "No!"

Might as well basket all your eggs in *isn't*,
Let warm illusion call your when and where.
That way our trash-heaps alchemize to Byzant
-ine dancing floors by gilt pavilions. There
Like lissom flora all an airy day
Plain Doe and 'Ligi to mad tambours sway.

Moses Descending

The burning questions of our time? They're burning,
That's all, as Troy did once. The ashes stay.
It's not with such concern our hearts are churning:
What moves the star by night, the sun by day
Hints at a primal *Why?* beyond the headlines,
Beyond the mole-eyed scientist's surmise.
Fiercer than any hunger in the breadlines,
To know! to know! is the hunger in our eyes.

But how? In a world by glutes and cleavage haunted,
Horoscope, crystal, junk bonds, fads and trends,
Gospel on T-shirts, string bikinis flaunted
To "make a statement." Moses, lo! descends,
Waves plastic tablets with gilt lettering:
"Good is what feels good, people. Do your thing!"

The Bathrobe

The bathrobe that you gave me, mischievous scarlet,
Slips from the hook. Retrieved again, goes slack.
I fumble, poke—the sleeves are where?—but snarl it,
Ram my fist in a pocket's cul-de-sac.

Unsnarl it, try again. Grope for the collar.
Collar? Or bottom hem? But now I deal
With a sash that tangles too, same devilish color.
This robe, it's all imbroglio! Makes me feel

I'm a lurching calf the novilleros harry
With crimson flurry of cape, like flaps I dance with.
I hang it up. It slinks to the floor, contrary.

Well, back to work, to cruxes I've a chance with:
Proton decay, weird pulsars, torques of G,
Fermat's last theorem, and lost symmetry.

As in a Play by Dekker

Instead of cobbling out my patchy verses
To catch your eye, I'd rather cobble—shoes!
Verse serves for—well, for what? It fills no purses;
In the world's strict accounting, pays no dues.
But shoes—there's substance for you! Given my druthers
I'd have a grubby shoeshop somewhere, rich
As musk with the sexy redolence of leathers,
Good goop, and the wily thread plied stitch on stitch,

And be a man then, not a pen. A proud one.
Each glossy pair, as promised, shelved on time.

You'd come for yours—best of the perks allowed one—
Plaid skirt aswirl in rhythm, knees in rhyme,
Lean close to me, palms fondling them, "Like new!"
My heart a wild thing as I'd breathe, "For you!"

Found Poem: Understanding the Universe

We're told how the great mazy world we wander
Was once a cozy garden we could tend:
Clouds snug above; the sun, the moon up yonder
Distant a piece, but neighborly, a friend.
But now, since Galileo—! Though the story's
On record, who can handle it? Let's say
Professor Plodd, his mind on inventories,
Amassed an *Atlas of the Milky Way*

—That single galaxy of heaven's zillion—
Giving a page, one page, to every star
(One to our sun and planets), some ten million
Volumes, each tombstone-size, would do. But are
There readers? Even to skim it would, one hears,
At a page a second, take ten thousand years.

Freight

... the world and all her train ...

—Henry Vaughan

I

Call Awe, then, what you will, long long ago
It set the heavenly Wheels in locomotion,
Lit stars to warn or beckon, set aflow
The salt of blood, express, from local ocean.
Soon man, with eye aglow and tongue that muttered,
(Banished from Eden's air? or pride of apes?)
Sat clinking flint on flint, and as they shattered
Snatched with a grin what fell in craftier shapes.

The law was move or die. Lively from tigers,
Dainty on deer. Survival called the tune.
Oxen, we learned, would bear us. So would rivers.
And that was science. On the whole a boon.
With hands that worried flint till tools accrue,
We tunneled mountains and rode cozy through.

II

We move, lock, stock, and barrel, all our store.
We *carry*—the word sings with care and courage!
The child, we say, is carried months before
It sees the sky. When grown, we approve its carriage.
True voices carry far; far voices ringing
Carry us back to an old Virginia dream.
The brave say, Carry on. Last, the low-swinging
Sweet chariot coming, for to carry us home.

Life's what we carry, as blood carries air.
Nations have lifeblood: the bright veins of steel
Carry in cars our treasure-trove and care—
Often survival rode the coupled wheel.
Men in the cave flaked stone, were learning how
They'd hew horizons into Here and Now.

III

Clouds are roulette-wheel of the heaven's weather;
The planets wheel, nightlong, in pride of place;
Wheels jewel the wrist, alert us: pain or pleasure;
—And one chilled-iron wheel confounded space.
What caveman on a round rock come a cropper
Rubbed at a rueful hip, brow furrowing *Why?*
Saw granite on loose gravel slip and quiver
Until—a dazzle of wheel-thought like sunrise!

History moved massive on that wheel, until
Boxcars, dark crimson as rich freighted blood,
Streamed from a central heart, made cities tall,
As if the very trains arose and stood
On end, tiered up together, scraping sky.
Pale gondolas of cloud go deadhead by.

IV

Set any wheel to earth, and two wheels meet:
Ours and the planet's ponderous wheel of stone
Rough with tectonic rubble, ridge and plate;
Yet both turn easy, like the wheels we've known.
Athens cut ruts of marble: ivory courses
Shunted Apollo's car of solar gold;
John Donne saw wagon-ways; the horse-power, horses.
Over the flats of Kansas sail-cars rolled.

First planks on yielding ground, then treads of metal,
Then steel set edgewise, over stone for ties.
A mountain? Sawtooth rail or crank-and-cable
Till iron took serene the incredulous rise.
Always a tingling rumor in the rail
Kept the one burden humming there: *Prevail.*

V

See the world pitched and tossed. The nerves of matter,
Tougher than cable, hawser hills in place.
Most stubborn stuff, it wills to cling together;
Huddling in love, won't slacken its embrace.
Move it we must though, chipping to our purpose
Irascible flint, blasting the mountain side;
Flexing the tensions our way or they warp us.
Time's a spring too; it tightens when denied.

Railroads, you toy with time, think time your bauble;
You run on time, shrink time, cut time in two.
Do time all kinds of wrong, bind *time* to *table*,
Brag that tomorrow is today for you.
Your goal: arrive—though heat, hail, heaven's fire
Snatch at the brass and varnish of the Flyer.

VI

Compleat with a nifty moniker, *Puffing Billy,*
Tom Thumb or *Rocket, General, Pioneer,*
Cycloped (horse on treadmill sweating), jolly
Sans Pareil, gloss and gold—they, year by year
Flew in the face of time and testy weather,
Enemies both, the lanterned trainmen know.
(By stoves where sand is baking crisp, they gather,
Trading the tall tales of high-striding snow.)

Through juniper in Utah, Pennsy tupelo,
Yucca round Tucson, tamarack in Vermont,
Engines with lamp, stack, bell—caboose with cupola—
Cowcatcher proud as Roman prow, they vaunt
Their way across the continent, huffy vassals
Hooting at towermen in their spidery castles.

VII

Best Friend of Charleston, Wabash Cannonball,
Are legend now; but emblems, gold and sable,
Recall them: beaver, mountain goat, the tall
Sequoia or snowy Shasta, robed in fable,
War bonnets of the Salt Lake Road, or torrid
Many-rayed sunset, blazoning their desire
To wrestle the jeweled tiara from Time's forehead,
Set records: *Express* or *Limited, Special, Flyer.*

In Promontory, Utah, '69,
The golden spike uniting East and West
Was sledged in creosote: high iron's sign,
Past roundhouse, shoo-fly shunting, toward their vast
Envisioning. And the spike held, tight as true
Fingers that lock in love and won't undo.

VIII

The lone prairie, the twilight gray as steel,
The vanishing freight—oh see the lonely road
Our fathers wandered, stumbling on the wheel,
—Daydreamers all, and the long row unhoed—
Sky-hankering men, their reverence still alive
Some years ago: with burning glass and sun
George Stephenson in 1825
Snatched fire for *Locomotion No. 1.*

Ten miles an hour, "immoderate" twelve—so once.
Slow Down to Ninety warns the black ravine.
Smoke-plumed, in armor, as with leveled lance
Engines career, as signals clear to green.
Time brought the caveman, chipper, all this way,
Far from the misty fens of yesterday.

Cultural Heritage

In the vast universe where star-worlds shatter,
These sages, saints, bards, tech-men—do they matter?
The best carve cherry-pits. The rest? They chatter.

Tandaradei!

Snowflake and rose. The surf at evening; wine:
Plaisir d'amour! All inklings? All a sign
No six-feet-under's stamped as bottom line?

Men's Room: The Ritz

Gold fixtures by Cellini and—look twice!—
Real ice cubes in the urinals. That's nice.
What's all earth's glory but a peeing on ice?

Trivia

> "... ἐν τριπλαῖς ἁμαξιτοῖς ..."
> —Oed. Tyr., 716

"Your verse—so trivial!"

Trivial? Of the street?
Trivial's *tri-via,* no? Where three roads meet,
And folks kiss, haggle, josh. Same bloody where
As Oedipus did in dad. You mean I'm there?

"Light" Verse

"Light verse!" Mamurra sniffed, "your whole damn
    batch."
Catullus packed iambics tight and "Catch!"
Grinned as he tossed them—*whoosh!*—they dumped
    like thunder
On—
        WHERE'S MAMURRA?
                Buried.
                      Six feet under.

Etymology

Prestige, we love it! But (pardon the intrusion)
It's from *prestigiæ,* Latin for *illusion,*
Or worse, *hoax, fraud,* plain *trickery.* Never mind,
Who love prestige won't check it. Love is blind.

Cajolery

Cajolery works, but you've got to know how.
Pulling its leg won't get milk from a cow.

You Pious People

Most any sin—read Scripture if you doubt it—
'S forgiven sooner than righteousness about it.

Horace, Ode I, 4

Blustery winter relents as we welcome the changing airs of springtime,
    And rollers trundle dried-out keels to harbor.
Cattle go free of their sheds and the farmer no longer hugs the fireside.
    No meadows glisten; blanching frosts are over.

Under the luminous moon, now the goddess of love directs her dancing,
    And shapely Graces, woodland nymphs assemble.
This ankle, that ankle gleams on the pulsating turf, and ruddy Vulcan
    Relights his forges for the waiting Cyclops.

Now is the time to entwine in our holiday hair a wreath of myrtle,
    Or strands of blossom open meadows lavish.
Now, in the shadowy groves, celebrations in gratitude to Faunus,
    His choice oblations, youngling goat or lambkin.

Pale Death pounds on the porch, chalks equally pauper's grubby hut and
    Great Caesar's palace. Lucky friend, remember:
Brief are the days of our life; no extravagant hopes for far tomorrows.
    The dark's upon us, all too soon—its phantoms,

Hades' impoverished house, stripped bare of amenities: no more your
    Old wining, dining, dancing days; no more your
Gazing at ivory limbs of that youngster his lusty fellows vie for
    This year, and next year all the girls are after.

Horace, Ode I, 5

Who's that slip of a boy, lotioned and soaped, who'll urge
Love on you in the cool grot by the rambling rose?
   Who've you tied back your golden
      Curls for, Pyrrha, in just your own

Simple elegant way? Oh what a shock in store
For him! "Count on the gods? Never again!" he'll groan,
   Dazed, ungainly, engulfed in
      Pitch-black hurricane-swirling seas.

Now he glories in you, thinking you purest gold;
Trusts you, "Always my own! Always my own true love!"
   Trusts you, never suspecting
      How torrential your summer air.

Those your glitter allures, put to no proof—beware!
I? Just made it to shore, hung up my storm-drenched clothes,
   Votive gifts for the shrine of
      Neptune, lord of the turning tide.

Catullus, XVII

O Colonia, mad to dance
                    all the length of your bridge, and
More than ready to do so now,
                    only fearful the trembly
Piers supporting the poor old thing's
                    salvaged rickety timbers
Might turn turtle and, wrong side up,
                    founder deep in the marshes—
Heaven grant you a better bridge,
                    true to specifications,
Where your Lords of the Dance, unharmed
                    can cavort in their orgies,
On condition you do one thing:
                    leave me doubled up, laughing,
When you collar this village fool,
                    plunge him—*plunk!*—in the thickest
Scummy muck underneath your bridge,
                    burbling, head over heels there.
But it's got to be where the bog's
                    grimmest guckiest gumbo
Stinks to heaven as nowhere else,
                    livid, color of corpses.
Him! He's dumbest of all dumb men.
                    See that tot in the cradle?
Two years old, but when half asleep
                    twice as bright as old stupor.
"Dumb? How so?" Well, his wife's a flower,
                    fresh in bloom, in her springtime,
No young creature as rare as she,
                    winning, warm—what a charmer!
Gardeners guarding their glossy grapes
                    needn't keep such an eye out
As that husband of hers—but no!
                    she's left free as a breeze to
Stray at will, and he doesn't blink,
                    doesn't budge, like a treetrunk

In a ditch where the logger's axe
    crippled, cropped, and forgot it.
There, unconscious of all, it lies,
    focused nowhere, on nothing.
This clod, stupor itself, is such:
    hears not, certainly sees not,
In a fog as to who he is,
    if he is, if he isn't.
He's the dummy I'd like to dunk
    upside down in your mudhole's
Dimmest depth, on the chance it might
    jolt him out of his coma,
Cling like glue to his sodden soul,
    leave it lodged in the wallow,
As the clutch of such yucky muck
    sucks the shoe from a jackass.

Catullus, XXV

You, swishy Timmie, softer stuff
          than plush of cuddly bunny,
Than goosey-gander's underfluff,
          than lovey-dovey earlobe,
Than old grandpappy's piddly part,
          in spider-webby squalor
—What's even worse: if any chest
          have chinks a-glint with treasure,
Then down you swoop, as whirlwinds whoosh,
          and snatch it up, and scuttle.
Example: take my Grecian robe
          (as take he did, did Timmie),
My napery crocheted in Spain,
          my knick-knacks from Bithynia.
Your conversation pieces now?
          "Old family things," you swagger?
Unglue them from your sticky mitts,
          and hand them over, stupid!
If not, you see these whips of ours?
          They'll sear with ruddy X's
Your palms that play at pat-a-cake,
          your little lambie bottom.
That's when you'll learn to twist and turn,
          like dinky dory bobbling
In boiling froth of outer banks,
          a crazy gale rampaging.

L'Infinito

Giacomo Leopardi

I always loved this solitary hill,
This hedgerow too, secreting from the view
So large a part of the far world's horizon.
But sitting here and gazing, in thought I conjure,
Beyond that hedge, the interminable tracts,
And silence more than man's, and peace so deep
The heart is all but daunted. And as I listen
To the wind at whisper in this foliage, so
That infinite silence to this very voice
I keep comparing, and there come to mind
Thoughts of *the eternal,* of old seasons dead,
And of ours now, vital, rife—the sound of it.
Amid this vastitude, all thought's awash:
And it's sweet to be lost in shipwreck on this sea.

Die schöne Nacht
Goethe

Now I leave the little cottage
Of my dearest; through the dark,
Secret, in a dreary silence,
Wander in the wooded park.
Luna peers though bush and oaktree
zephyr makes her coming known;
Birches bow; they strew a fragrance
On the winds of midnight blown.

What a pleasure in the coolness
Of so rich a summer night!
What a hush! The feeling spirit
Revels in untold delight.
Rapture I can hardly cope with,
Nights of secrecy astir,
Yet, I'd trade them, by the thousand,
For a single night with her.

"Cando Penso Que Te Fuches . . ."
Rosalía de Castro

When I think you gone, abruptly
It begins again, the haunting.
Dark penumbra that benumbs me,
Round my bed you circle, taunting.

When again I think you absent,
In the dark your shadow masses;
And you're somber in the starlight,
Somber in the wind that passes.

Any song I hear, you sing it;
You're the mourner in all mourning;
You're the brook, its doleful murmur;
You're the dead of night, the dawning.

You're my all. My all and only.
Round me, in me, leaving never.
Dark penumbra that benumbs me,
You're my very self forever.

FIVE YOUNG AMERICAN POETS

1944

Dollar Bill

The feathered thing of silver-gray and jade,
Her wing with sum and pompous annal spread,
Is strangest bird, world's wonder. Of more than stork
Or dove or jay or any eagle bred.
Her silver eggs explode with wine or milk,
Gardenia, limousine, or firework silk.

Her nature wild. Once captured, not a bird,
Heron nor Persian lark, is fed so fine.
Her Audubon, the banker, stalks and peers
Where audits bloom and grills of commerce twine.
She lives in leather nest or cote of steel.
In city migrates on the armored wheel.

Mallard and teal the fowler downs in fall.
But season is open always for green game.
All weapons used: hand or enchanting hair,
Instructed dice or dynamite or flame.
To pipe of organ some in chapel tread;
Others in alley with a pipe of lead.

Nameless. Her whims of voyage none can track.
Her legend lost; perhaps is charm or curse.
From chaw-stained overall she flutters straight
To the sweet nonsense of a lady's purse.
Wanton with rouge, with blood and beer defiled,
Is loved at Christmas by the snowy child.

She teems in steeple wall, or no bells ring;
In clinic roof, or all the patients die;
She lies with laurel on the captain's head
Or nations fall; their banners leave the sky.
Strange bird. Strange music from the poison breath.
Child of green lovebird and the raven death.

Penny Arcade

This pale and dusty palace under the El
The ragged bankers of one coin frequent,
Beggars of joy, and in a box of glass
Control the destiny of some bright event.
Men black and bitter shuffle, grin like boys,
Recovering Christmas and elaborate toys.

The clerk controls the air gun's poodle puff
Or briefly the blue excalibur of a Colt,
Sweeps alien raiders from a painted sky,
And sees supreme the tin flotilla bolt.
Hard lightning in his eye, the hero smiles,
Steady MacArthur of the doodad isles.

The trucker arrogant for his Sunday gal
Clouts the machine, is clocked as "Superman!"
The stunted negro makes the mauler whirl
Toy iron limbs; his wizen features plan
The lunge of Louis, or, no longer black,
Send to the Pampas battering Firpo back.

Some for a penny in the slot of love
Fondle the bosom of aluminum whores,
Through hollow eye of lenses dryly suck
Beatitude of blondes and fallen drawers.
For this Cithaeron wailed and Tempe sighed,
David was doomed, and young Actaeon died.

Who gather here will never move the stars,
Give law to nations, track the atom down.
For lack of love or vitamins or cash
All the bright robins of their year have gone.
Here heaven ticks: the weariest tramp can buy
Glass mansions in the juke-seraphic sky.

The Genuine Ellis

The soul too is dragged by the body into the region of the changeable,
wanders and is confused; the world spins round her, and she is like a
drunkard when she touches change

—Plato

One thought is all the burden of our learning:
What is and what is not.
For this
The kindergarten shines at first communion
And the slugged goon is shot.
The broker yachts the Florida wave. Slum-fevered
The lungs of lovers rot.

Local Boy, Nine, Swims Lake. Hits Fortieth Homer.
Wins All-American Rate.
Condescends to coke, revered; and lolls at many
A moonlit gate.
Desires
One girl—and a highschool teacher marries
That nextdoor date.

A Phi Beta Kappa sops head in a desperate ointment;
Is bald as a toad.
Morbid, reads stoic Plutarch, dotes on a razor;
One day
Digs at his throat.
Is alarmed at the speed of blood, swabs iodine, sobbing:
"Hell of a note."

Encircling our Coney shore the waded oceans
Loiter and loot.
And out of sky, abrupt on a pleasant evening,
The riddled airmen chute.
Through autumn of blood advances the lonely hunter
With brutal boot.

The dunce world, capped with day, with darkness
    trousered,
Is to this college brought,
To learn:
Love is, or it isn't love, and what is?
Mind errs and flesh is flogged. Passion is taught
To build igloos of the icy cubes of concept,
Ergo and ought.

We, seasick, leap to land from the reeling scupper;
Love sun, being bred of night;
Endure
Our inky earth eclipsed from a sun off somewhere,
Fearfully bright.
Who shall know as we, we duped, the genuine Ellis,
Island of light?

Magazine Stand

Here shines the grotto of our lacquered saints.
Their locks are lightning and their eye a knife.
They and the flooded angels who see God
Alone take straight the stinging scotch of life.
They stride the world, gather with magic glove
War's angry garland or the flowers of love.

Here in the urns and roses of the garden,
Her finger in the rites of nicotine,
Beauty is dreaming in her chlorine tresses,
And pastry angels of the cinema lean.
Here Petty's queen, the madonna of the lathe,
Is chaired with the naked saints that grin and bathe.

In nickel pots of paper, knighthood flowers:
Cowboys are riled and beautiful with wounds;
Plummet to earth hyena-men from Mars;
The princess in delicious torture swoons;
And a blonde the nazis know with tapping hand
Panics the sanctum of the high command.

A college too: for boys and popeyed scholars
The virgin tables of all knowledge lie,
The roisterous catalogue of sport or sex
And how to dance or in five lessons fly.
For deeper mind, the planets' stolen codes
And what the dragon of the zodiac bodes.

Mont-Saint-Michel of pulp on every corner
Climbing the sky, vermilion, gold, and green,
Is shrine of our ideal and perhaps holy,
The taste of God being wry and absinthe-keen:
His favorite toy the lamb with broken spring;
His favorite singer the adulterous king.

Madrigal in Wartime

Beside the rivers of the midnight town
Where four-foot couples love and paupers drown,
Shots of quick hell we took, our final kiss,
The great and swinging bridge a bower for this.

Your cheek lay burning in my fingers' cup;
Often my lip moved downward and yours up
Till both adjusted, tightened, locksmith-true:
The flesh precise, the crazy brain askew.

Roughly the train with grim and piston knee
Pounded apart our pleasure, you from me;
Flare warned and ticket whispered and bell cried.
Time and the locks of bitter rail divide.

For ease remember, all that parted lie:
Men who in camp of shot or doldrum die,
Who at land's-end eternal furlough take

—This for memento as alone you wake.

Scherzo: Writers' Conference, 1941

Satire, the sultry lady, is my love.
Her eyes are clear; her kiss, precision-sweet.
And now her latest law: to leer at those
Who here for sentiment or fashion meet,
At bards who chat a while because it pays them.
I come to bury these and not to praise them.

Hither the local poet, champ of rime,
Advances, hugs a folder full of dreams.
He struts, aware of height and manly tan
And laurelled in the latest color-schemes.
Some figure he! would stable, if he could,
His rakish Pegasus at Hollywood.

And here our aunts and neighbors, lush with lace,
(Who should be home and putting up preserves)
Collapse and let the fingers of cool art
Massage again their fact-afflicted nerves.
As they adjust their psyches and their hats,
They lap the milk of beauty up like cats.

These solemn men, who tread the holy grass
And, warm in tweed, ooze poetry and sweat,
Rooster the flock; in scrawny nests of fame
They on the eggs of ancient counsel set.
"Soak self in loveliness" is doubtless fine—
Dante was soaked in God; Catullus, wine.

This poetry, austere and cunning brute,
Scours on fierce wing the loneliest sky above,
Prowls with black paw himalayas of the soul,
Lurks with hot eye in the dank wood of love.
Think twice before you take this beast to bed:
They find you in the morning raped and dead.

New Year's Eve

Midnight the years last day the last
high hour the verge where the dancers comet
(loved water lapsing under the bridge
and blood dear blood by the bridged aorta
where the dreaming soul leans distant-eyed
long-watching the flood and its spoil borne seaward)

and I one fleck on the numbered face
one dot on the star-aswarming heaven
stand here in this street of all our streets
of all our times this moment only
the bells the snow the neon   faces
each our own but estranged and fleeing

from a bar all tinkle and red fluorescence
a boy in a tux with tie uneven
puppy-clumsy with auldlangsyning
plaintive so droll came crying Sally
Salleee again and Saalleee louder
a violin teased   he passed in laughter

yet under the heart of each up vein
up brain and loud in the lonely spirit
a-rang desire for Sallys name
or another name or a street or season
not to be conjured by any horn
nor flavored gin nor the flung confetti

o watcher upover the world look down
through gale of stars to the globes blue hover
and see arising in troubled mist
from firefly towns and the dark between them
the waif appeal from lackland hearts
to Sallys name or perhaps anothers

we shall never be never be calm not we
who have seen for an instant you   you standing
at night in the cloudlit rose of cities
or underblue of a womans lashes
crying where   we wandered veldt and highland
drift and doom were the loves we lovered

Prayer

We who are nothingness can never be filled:
Never by orchards on the blowing sea,
Nor the rich foam of wheat all summer sunned.

Our hollow is deeper far than treasure can fill:
Helmets of gold swim ringing in the wells
Of our desire as thimbles in the sea.

Love cannot fill us either: children's love,
Nor the white care of mothers, nor the sweet
Concem of sister nor the effort of friends;

No dream-caress nor actual: the mixed breath,
Lips that fumble in dark and dizzily drink
Till all nerves tighten to the key of love.

The feasted man turns empty eyes about;
The king builds higher on a crumbling base,
His human mouth a weapon; his brain, maps.

The lover wakes in horror: he gropes out
For the known form, and even enfolding, fears
A bed by war or failing blood undone.

For we who are nothingness can nothing hold.

Only solution: come to us, conceiver,
You who are all things, held and holder, come to us;
Come like an army marching the long day
And the next day and week and all that year;

Come like an ocean thundering to the moon,
Drowning the sunken reef, mounting the shore.
Come, infinite answer to our infinite want.

Her ancient crater only the sea can fill.

Parting: 1940

Not knowing in what season this again
Not knowing when again the arms outyearning
Nor the flung smile in eyes not knowing when

Not sure beyond all doubt of full return
Not sure of time now nor the film's reversal
This all done opposite, the waif regathered

Like our lost parents in the blinded song
We bag in hand with wandering steps and slow
Through suburbs take our solitary way

Not that all clouds are garrisoned and stung
Not that horizons loom with coppered legions
Not that the year is dark with weird condition

All who parted in all days looked back
Saw the white face, the waving. And saw the sea
Not knowing in what season this again

For well they knew, the parters in all evenings
Druid and Roman and the rocked Phoenician:
The blood flows one imposed way, and no other

from

THE IRON PASTORAL

1947

Love Poem

My clumsiest dear, whose hands shipwreck vases,
At whose quick touch all glasses chip and ring,
Whose palms are bulls in china, burs in linen,
And have no cunning with any soft thing

Except all ill-at-ease fidgeting people:
The refugee uncertain at the door
You make at home; deftly you steady
The drunk clambering on his undulant floor.

Unpredictable dear, the taxi drivers' terror,
Shrinking from far headlights pale as a dime
Yet leaping before red apoplectic streetcars—
Misfit in any space. And never on time.

A wrench in clocks and the solar system. Only
With words and people and love you move at ease;
In traffic of wit expertly manoeuvre
And keep us, all devotion, at your knees,

Forgetting your coffee spreading on our flannel,
Your lipstick grinning on our coat,
So gayly in love's unbreakable heaven
Our souls on glory of spilt bourbon float.

Be with me, darling, early and late. Smash glasses—
I will study wry music for your sake.
For should your hands drop white and empty
All the toys of the world would break.

Midwest

Indiana: no blustering summit or coarse gorge;
No flora lurid as disaster-flares;
No great vacuities where tourists gape
Nor mountains hoarding their height like millionaires.
More delicate: the ten-foot knolls
Give flavor of hill to Indiana souls.

Topography is perfect, curio-size;
Tidy as landscape in museum cases.
What is beautiful is friendly and underfoot,
Not flaunted like theater curtains in our faces.
No peak or jungle obscures the blue sky;
Our land rides smoothly in the softest eye.

Man is the prominent fauna of our state.
Elsewhere circus creatures stomp and leer
With heads like crags or clumps. But delirious nature
Once in a lucid interval sobering here
Left (repenting her extravagant plan)
Conspicuous on our fields the shadow of man.

Christmas Tree

This seablue fir that rode the mountain storm
Is swaddled here in splints of tin to die.
Sofas around in chubby velvet swarm;
Onlooking cabinets glitter with flat eye;
Here lacquer in the branches runs like rain
And resin of treasure starts from every vein.

Light is a dancer here and cannot rest.
No tanagers or jays are half so bright
As swarms of fire that deep in fragrance nest
In jungles of the gilt exotic night
Where melons hang like moonstone. White above
Rises that perfect star, the sign of love.

On carpets' fairy turf, in rainbow dark,
Here once the enchanted children laid their heads,
Reached for the floating moon above the park,
And all their hopes were simple blues and reds.
Beneath the electric halo, none could see
Swords in the ankle of the victim tree.

Each named a patron star: Arthur said green
For August in the country; and Betty blue
For swinging and the Florida surf; while Jeanne
Decided gold. One horoscope was true:
The star of Donald low and lava-red—
Enlisted Donald, in Australia dead.

Our lives were bound to sorcery and night.
Zodiacs crumble on the boughs of rust
For every child is gone. Some burned too bright
And now lie broken in the bins of dust;
And some, a fortunate few, adventured far
And found assurance in the perfect star.

Trainwrecked Soldiers

Death, that is small respecter of distinction,
Season or fitness, in an instant these
Tan casual heroes, floral with citation,
Scattered for blocks over the track
In lewd ridiculous poses, red and black.

These had outfaced him in the echoing valleys;
Thwarted like men of stone incredible fire;
Like dancers had evaded the snub bayonet;
Had ridden ocean or precipitous air.
Death turned his face aside, seemed not to see.
His unconcern made boyish melodrama
Of all that sergeant threatened, corporal bore,
Or captain shouted on the withering shore.

He watched the newsreel general pinning on their
Blouses the motley segments of renown;
Stood patient at the cots of wounded
Where metal pruned and comas hung;
Nodded to hear their plans: one with a child
His arms had never held; one with a bride;
One with a mere kid's longing for the gang
In green and ticking poolroom bluff with beer.
All these he herded through sargasso of mines
Back to the native field and Sunday steeple
Where only the russet hunters late in fall
Nitre the frosty heaven with abrupt smoke.
There he arose full height, suddenly spoke.

Spoke, and the four dimensions rocked and shattered;
Rearing, the olive pullmans spun like tops;
Corridors shrank to stairway and shot up;
Window, green pastoral lately, turned grenade;
The very walls were scissor and cut flesh.
Captain and sergeant tumbled, wholly void
Their muscle, fortitude, and khaki fame
Like rules intended for another game.

Then death, the enormous insolence effected,
The tour de force pat and precisely timed,
Resumes his usual idiom, less florid:
A thousand men are broken at Cologne;
Elderly salesman falters on the landing;
Girl Slain in Park; Plane Overdue; Tots Drown.
But we who walk this track, who read, or see
In a dark room the shaggy films of wreck—
What do the carrion bent like letters spell
More than the old *sententiae* of chance?—
Greek easier (αἴλινον αἴλινον) than this fact.
You lie wry X, poor men, or empty O,
Crux in a savage tongue none of us know.

Sign of Fever

Toys that parting lovers give
We gave, and gave each other too,
Novice in the knack of love.
Rose or ring would better do,
    But soul was soaring, eagle-wild;
    Body was a tagging child.

Where the sign of fever burns
Caller's car is rarely seen;
So our blood from public care
Writes immortal quarantine.
    Long as neuron's annal last,
    Each is in the other lost.

Lover, on the southern wave
Cruise, inviting sleep again.
I along the winter fields
Straggle with the midland men.
    Skull's a shut and haunted room.
    Dream of each is other's doom.

A FOUNTAIN IN KENTUCKY

1950

The Masque of Blackness

> The first face of the *Scene* appeared all obscure, & nothing perceiv'd but
> a darke Rocke, with trees beyond it; and all wildnesse, that could be
> presented; Till, at one corner of the cliffe, above the *Horizon* the *Moone*
> began to shew. . . .

I

The news stirred first in very dead of winter:
A rumor of new breathing by late spring,
New lungs for the world's air, planets' new center,
New eyes brimming new colors—a new everything!
The ticking kaleidoscope rearranged its tenses;
The present faded; future's the true noon.
As both the man and woman grew new senses
They laughed at sun, set all their dials by Soon.

The streets and rooms they moved in rang unreal
Since not yet real to the child; say someone's dream
Strange as drowned cities where the cursive eel
Flashes in alleys. A curtain-time scene:
Whether they shifted vases, turned a page,
All seemed last-minute touches on a stage.

II

The stage and a man's life—long before Avon
Cynical Palladas saw we "play a part."
Though of that scenery or the gapes it gave on—
Hard to say which is model and which art.
Down the steep aisles of a murky vast
Theater, all seats empty, he and she
Go groping backstage; from a passionate past
Glitter the lurid flats of cloud and sea.

On one dark door a blurred name and a star;
Many costumes: banker, burglar, streaming sheik;
Many props: sword, castle, couch, arrogant car,
High enough balconies to break a neck.

He sits down, a most "practicable" bed;
She feels a dagger and the edge runs red.

III

Up with the drowsy curtain! No more slumber—
Hear the telephone dinning at midnight in the west?
The far-off hospital nudging his number:
The baby is born sooner than they guessed.
O thousand miles of wire, you may well be humming
To tractors and farms and fences and silos and
    signboards and, well,
Say to those huddled towns, say: Someone's coming:
Out with your bunting; bang on that firebell.

But in deserted halls of the long dorm
Corners piled with luggage jostle and sigh.
The window faint in lightning is breathing warm.
And look: pandemonium in the sky
As moons (a trick of tears) are bobbing in tens;
Each star is twenty stars! What a wild lens!

IV

In the cradle, furled, unfurled, anemone fingers
Stir celluloid susurrus and pink chime;
How they shall hook *him* where he brags and lingers,
Old mustache-tugging, flint, foreclosing Time.
Let him rasp let him grin let him wheedle:
    must disgorge.
Palms must twist up, slow-open tense as traps
Restoring coins, curls, girls in the Greek surge,
And tears that fell pitting forlorn war-maps.

Then yours (anemone) rain-wandering panes
All joy at dusk; the Magi's intense shed;
Skill with a knife, decision, trucks and cranes;

Tall midnight prodding many a guess at God—
That love that moves the sun. From love you are;
O plunge unaging in the enraging star!

V

A six-month-old discoverer, this baby
Goggles for days at his elate right hand
Till his head falters and blue eyes blur. Maybe
He gurgles an off-vowel sound, nodding bland.
Then the hand hovers, sways like a pink flower—
What will you do with it turned brusque and human?
Half floral and half bird no more—tweed power,
Wristwatch-consulter and cigared acumen?

On keyboard, dashboard, surfboard, labor-relations
        board
O use it better than we, your likely future:
Manage for human hope earth's pirate hoard
And trick the tumblers of combustible nature.
Or, mildlier made, project us. Call desire
Two cups on midnight throw-rugs by the fire.

VI

One day they learned that sorrow wore old tweed,
That lounging disaster spoke a soft hello.
Not where the wounds of wreck or battle bleed
But in the dullish office you all know.
Many searchlights locked and rusted on that scene
Throw blacker shapes than noon: there the child lies;
Doctors are curt, averted; what they mean
Concern shows livelier in the mother's eyes.

In her tight fingers round a rubber lamb
She brought to show them all: See he can play.

Now if calamity with his drunkard's aim,
Or grief with minimizing hands—if they
Edge up or shriek in the shrubs—no gasp, no start:
This is one routine they know by heart.

VII

Confronting that fact's what-about-it shrug
In a mist of danker friends and family,
They started to take metaphor like a drug,
To lay on open wounds emollient simile.
As: tears are the best lens for seeing sky,
Or: that bluesteel thunder clears the air.
But when alone they sobered, eye to eye,
The big skywriting withered, wasn't there.

What was? Why some irrelevance and flummery:
They noted eyes blurred less in blurring rain,
That cheeks flushed in the snow at least—in summary
Though past and future's gone, some Now remains.
No mountain blazing candid, no, not one—
They picked up pebbles and these argued stone.

VIII

(Antimasque)

Because someone was gone, they bought a dog,
A collie pup, black, orange, flashy white.
He gnawed on table legs, troubled the rug;
His growls and pokings varied the empty night.
Except for that red flopping tongue, a fawn.
Intense but scattering, coffee-eyed. At play
White as piano keys on the green lawn
His paws improvised snatches of ballet.

(The grinning show that Must Go On; the voice
Without past, without future, crying rejoice.)

This dog, this gawk, this zealot of frivolity,
Bounding assiduous sniffer hung with hair—
What could a romping fetish of this quality
Do in that house, with that shadow there?
Oh nothing. They knew that. The insane dancer
Was queried: Dance Dance was all the answer.

IX

One day they made the abandoned beach their home
—The sky electric-blue, sea dark as plum—
And watched the ivory spindles of the foam
Shaped by curved chisels and a big windy thumb.
They loved it here, and would have—none of that!
Rusty with sand the near-in waves grate *no;*
The folly-printed shore utters *no* flat;
Wave erasing wave erasing wave shakes *no.*

   (Above, the clouds' untidy pompous scrawl
   Means *no* if it means anything at all.)

More *no*'s flurry the mind than gulls that view.
He stared till italics teased him in the spray
(This lettered man), saw waves scrawl *W*
Stubbornly, turning *no* to *now;* saw *K*
In caving slant of breakers. New winds blow:
With every *K* imploding, *now* was *know.*

X

Know? But know what? Addenda from such minus?
Any true time from clock hands so bent back?
A city from ruins—
Once crystal halls now staring hollow and black?
Two cups all seesaw splinters, telephone's tremor,
Hard Time foreclosing on what appeared free?—
As (almost obscene memento of summer)
A white dog dances by the terrible sea.

Well, they know this: the cloud-ornate proscenium
Where Space-Time whirs a gilt rococo cage
With clowns and cats performing—no millennium
Here. They observed from many-roped backstage
And clanking cellarage. But admired much art,
Seeing the works of the bright world apart.

The Indolent Day

Today went meaningless as music.
Variations in the key of rain.
Even the street of hard curbs and porches
Sang in the whirling and pour of the pane.

Was scherzo in the dime-store red as a fire truck.
In the park was adagio and dripping green.
Sloshed in the rubble alley, aqua funebre.
Gasped sostenuto at any machine.

Having all day no wisdom weighed or spoken,
A sheepish no-good I lie alone,
My veins a-humming yet, like violin strings,
A fife or froggy bassoon in every bone.

Exulting: it might have had other relations and
    intervals,
Been in some exotic scale and not this one
Of affectionate Re, green Mi, history of Sol-fa
Twined in the minor rain, the dominant sun.

City Dawn

First breath of dawn, that corroborates all fable:
All we wanted in fairytale, is true.
Remember the scene: squires Maying under the
    pennoned castle?
Grass is that green, heaven that storybook-blue.

No domes of Mecca here, those rainbow bubbles.
No tricks of Gothic lightning amazing the sky.
Apartments climb in the clouds, and Sunday pavements
Broader than ballrooms of any Louis lie.

Or is it not steel, not stone, but our own blood
Filling these shapes, as air the vivid balloon?
Raising the intricate skyline miles away,
Floating even the sun toward hover of noon?

Over coffee and fruit such assurance of power
That the heart and the tear ducts choke: too much
    delight—
Returned to the world of solids and positive tread
After the howling mirrors, the chutes and loons of the night.

Though the morning paper cry black and squarely Woe
As planes lock, senators jangle, cottages bobble in flood,
There gathers a joy that is not quite lost all day
As we prove *to be, to know* in our warm blood.

The Bright Night of the Soul

Cool clarinet, bluff trumpet
Cajoling, sweet and mean,
Though lense of raised martini
Your swaying wraith was seen.

Came closer, was embodied.
No rest for either then.
Gaze with gaze bantered, far from
The icecube-clinking men.

Our soft-talk, gears engaging,
Moved smoother, glance by glance,
On barstools, while the dicecup
Played at love's grander dance.

Chrome, neon, barglass sparkled,
Were jeweled Aladdin-lands.
Time stopped at *now*. Our watches
Cried *Alas* for their lost pretty hands,

Till chairs scrambled silly on tables,
The yawning musicians were gone.
We in the door staring at
Tall astonishing dawn;

We in the park staring
Soon at the sun hours up,
At day's routine seen plain in
Dregs of the coffee cup.

Then we were glum. So many
Surly *perhapses* crowd
Deep in the deacon's adage,
Black in the bomber's cloud.

Although . . . what if . . . supposing . . .
But hesitations quailed
When, as in shining armor,
Nevertheless prevailed,

Prevailed against *whatever*!
All bids, all ante's met.
That week. That month. That summer.
Irrefutable yet.

Nevertheless, our gauntlet.
One bright night of the soul
Come fair, come foul, stays haloed,
Polaris at the Pole.

Watcher Go Deftly

Careful, careful; you cannot be too deft
With the pines on the shore and the little shells
Lip-color, eyelid-color, pale as a thigh—
Feel your palm tingle with little gourds and bells?

Especially you are dumb brother seaweed's keeper;
Nobody likes him—clutch, a rubber glove.
This, and all moon-crater gates of crawfish
Look at with love.

Curious chain mail of atoms underfoot,
Pandora's box too fine for fumbling—much
Of this you can penetrate, being careful
With that combustible touch.

But all those girls that kneel to collect shells,
Then straighten, thin girls, swinging back their hair,
That soft explosive fire. Watcher go deftly,
Is there in earth or heaven enough care?

First Date

Her toe first in that water
To which all walkers come
(Not Charon his blunt ferry
Creaks with more travelers home),
She stands, gasping in moonlight,
Never again the same.

Never the girl her mother
Patted pink-ribboned to school;
Never again her daddy's
Oops-a-daisy doll.
And the herons and gulls of the picnic beach
Shrink to a small role.

Shyly your ankle, Sharon,
Gamely, shin and knee
Tingle and chill, go under—
Then you begin to know.
The dark waves wash to your waist and
Ah there is no help now

From us on the snug pavilion
With paper lanterns lit,
As, deep in the dark we stare on,
The breakers chalk on slate
Tristan . . . Iseult . . . accountings
The children heed too late.

Japanese Prints

These took the captain prisoner that took these.
He had blown their homes ramshackle as their syllabary,
Found in the rubble this book, opened it—
In storm clouds, a blue porthole on serenity.

The two-inch craftsmen, intense ivory faces,
Worked in their beamed and linen-colored courtyards:
The bender of bows with his long black
    bow-shaped mustache;
Weavers (two women watched, their intricate hair
Like crullers lacquered); the old utensil-maker,
Pots all around—that picture clanked and glimmered.

Pictures: lenses. See more seeing less,
Seeing this page the sky blows. So this soldier
Took Japan with him, knew his heart Japan:
Japan first pointed his own street and people.

Incident

Our cinder kitten with violet eyes
Yesterday crept under couches, wouldn't be seen.
At dawn she was dead by the door.

The event was petty; its impetus not.

The orange setter paws her; rearing snorts,
Mills off wild as a wagon-wheel broke loose.

We who this first winter far from town
Walk in the ornate snow and love each other,
Sensible people, never weep for kittens
(Their wide-eyed acrobatics up the banister;
Their witty meetings with rubber mice).

But wading this afternoon in upblown drift
By the lank fences, each one hides
What he hopes the other has not seen: conjecture's
Ragged feather bloodied in the snow.

Winter in the Park

Lagoons are shrunk and walkable as concrete,
The little islands accessible now
That in June were a green secret the sunburnt lovers
Bumped with their rented prow.

Trees empty and fibrous, as if their roots were in air
By the sidewalk burled with ice
Where concessions huddle boarded, nothing to sell.
Oh how it was shady and nice

In easy July, in the ice-cream days, the lazy
Lying in sunhot grass we two;
The creak and bobble of rowing, the dusty scuff
And stare in the barbarous zoo:

Where lions lay bearded like Holbeins and polar
    bears clowned;
Where Jumbo waved sousaphone trunk;
The black leopard circled in whirlwind with flashlight for eyes;
Kangaroos hopped erotic and drunk.

Ape, tiger, swan (child's graphic A B C)
Spelled *us* then, spelled our rage and play.
Now the violent nursery is numb under snow;
The playthings all put away.

Vicarage Blues

I was not aboard when the big boat sunk;
I was not in the overturned car.
But I stood on the bank, I stood on the curb,
Frozen for those who were

Till chairs were floating around my neck;
I was upside down in the car.
Men on the shore and the curious curb—
None could think of a cure.

Many a coral girl on the boat;
Many a boy in the car.
As mother, mentor, motorman watch
Ended is all that care.

Ended the blanket tucked at night;
The songs of the caroling car.
Life that flushed as an apple once
Shatters white to the core.

Treasure of curl on the luxury boat;
Treasure of arm in the car.
Night and day dice it away—
Carol and coral and cure.

Two Cretan Views

Crete, forty centuries ago.
An afternoon like yesterday
Where, in the mazes of blunt brick,
Sun on the jigsaw gardens lay.

And Minos under a pink and lime
Windy canopy yawned at ease,
Laughed as his cup-chill fingers drew
A girl's white throat to his sunburnt knees.

Minoan boys in the court below
Flashy as dancers, forelocks blown,
Tease a red lackadaisical bull—
Vaulting sharp pendulums of bone;

One eye on the tall girls, two or three,
Who, walking a fawn, laugh taunting praise,
Bright lips arching the kiss-shape cry
(For thick with theta the Cretan phrase).

Servants conduct through the halls
With bull and acrobat glazed
A tiptoeing stranger, wary of eye
In that rumble of corridors—amazed.

A shipwrecked man from the dour north
Where indigo rocky headlands jut—
Forearm corded, salt with the oar,
Craggy of forehead, taut of gut;

A swarthy imaginative man,
That, frozen, stares through a hoarse door
At twisted limbs' contortion in air,
Flaring snout of the Mino-taur,

A rustle of maidens pale in shade,
Red tassels shook from a wild horn.
Fiercely he breaks and flees.

So the great bugaboo is born.

Portrait

Seeing in crowded restaurants the one you love
You wave at the door, tall girl in imperious fur,
And make for him, bumping waiters, dropping a glove,
Arriving soft with affectionate slur.
As ladies half-turn, gazing, and men appraise
You heap the linen with purse, scarf, cigarettes, lighter,
Laughing some instantaneous droll phrase.
As if sudden sun came out, the table is brighter.

All moods: at a party everybody's delight;
Intent while brown curls shadow the serious page;
When people are stuffy (more correct than right)
The stamp and turn on heel of a little girl's rage.
But woman mostly, as winter moonlight sees,
Impetuous midnight, and the dune's dark trees.

The Child

How the greenest of wheat rang gold at his birth!
How oaks hung a pomp in the sky!
When the tiptoeing hospital's pillowy arms
Godsped him in suns of July.

Then dizziest poplars, green-and-white tops,
Spun spinning in strings of the wind,
As that child in his wicker
With two great safeties pinned

Slept twenty-two hours with a Buddha-fine face
(His hands were palm-up like a dancer's).
Or his tragic mask's sudden pink-rubbery woe
Sent us thumbing four books for the answers.

And the grave clouds smiled over,
Smiled, flowing west to east, countering sun;
Fields at their leaving all spurted up green!
Old fences limped by at a run!

O elms, fling up up up corinthian fountains.
Fields, be all swirl and spangle: tangle of mirth—
Soon you will root in his woodbrook eyes more deeply
(O reborn poplars) than in Michigan earth.

Christmas

They say: but cattle near
And the infant in harsh hay!
Indeed harsh: how could honest God
Be man another way?

By lying lax in gold
Near many a bent knee?
Bedded in bright percent and so
Vouching hypocrisy?

Oh man's-flesh is most really this:
A thin cry in the cold;
Dust made a little while aware,
Shriveled both young and old.

When infants are born rich
The gaudy zoos troop in:
The elephant with button eyes;
The tiger, springs of tin.

And friends and relatives gape,
A simple clucking clan.
More honest—no?—when Bethlehem
Told the home-truth of man.

Adam's Ballad

"So sweetly bedded in Being,
So lost in locks of the sun;
So flushed and dazzled by dawn, by
Dark so troubled and spun.

"Bold in the owner's region,
I who have no right here
Have taken Being, his lady,
Slept with his wayward dear.

"Drunk the shy mist, her kisses,
On her wild breasts floated, the sea,
As heaven, bluest eye burning,
Was bending only on me.

"Part of his white love's body
God shall not have again.
He let me in and I took her.
She will stay among men.

"Even God, beholding bright Esse,
Trembles in rage of delight.
What of me, who fast in her forearms
Share the deep of the night?"

Thus as the blood rose warmer
Was Adam's saga begun—
So sweetly bedded in Being,
So lost in locks of the sun.

from

KNOWLEDGE OF THE EVENING

1960

The Evergreen

Under this stone, what lies?
   A little boy's thistledown body.
How, on so light a child
   Gravel hefted and hurled?
Light? As a flower entwined
   In our shining arms. Heavy
Laid in this scale—it set
   Wailing the chains of the world.

b.

What did you say? We said:
   Bedtime, dear, forever.
Time to put out the light.
   Time for the eyes to close.
What did he do? He lay
   In a crazyquilt of fever.
His hands were already like grasses.
   His cheek already a rose.

c.

How was that year? His voice.
   Over sun on the rug, slow-turning,
Hung like a seabird lost the
   Lorn and bodiless cry.
Haunting the house. *And then?*
   I remember *then.* One morning
Silence like knives in the ear.
   A bird gone over the sea.

d.

What of his eyes? Dark glow
   Furling the world's great surface.
Bubbles among tree lights;
   Bubbles of ferny dew.

And his kiss? On our cheek at evening
　　Vintage: a fine bursting.
This, and never dreamed his
　　Span was a bubble too?

e.

Little head, little head,
　　Frail in the air, gold aster—
Why did the great king stoop
　　And smoothe those ringlets down?
For a tinsel party-hat?
　　It was Christmas then, remember?
I remember grown men wept
　　And couldn't lift that crown.

f.

Mother, these tears and tears?
　　The better to see you, darling.
Mother, your golden glasses—
　　Have a sorry fault,
Being made for things, dear,
　　Mostly: carts and marbles.
Mothers wear, for children,
　　Better the stinging salt.

g.

What you remember most—?
　　Is a way of death with fingers.
How they are cast in tallow
　　—Fingers, webbed as one.
Where was he going, with webs?
　　A flying child? or a swimming?
He knew, where he went,
　　One way back to the sun.

h.

"Tesoro!" implored the maid.
    "Treasure!" the tall signora.
Under a distant heaven
    What struck the famous tower?
Faults in the earth despairing.
    Worlds away, an orchard
Offered violets early.
    And we returned a flower.

i.

Where does he lie? Hill-high
    In a vision of rolling river.
Where the dogwood curls in April
    And June is a dream of Greece.
Like a Christmas scene on china,
    Snow and the stubborn myrtle.
Those flakes from feathery heaven—?
    Deepen all in peace.

j.

Where does he rest, again?
    In a vision of rolling river.
What does he know of river?
    What do we know of sea?
Comfort?—when tomorrow's
    Cheek by jowl with never?
Never . . . in whose garden
    Bloomed the used-to-be.

k.

Under the snow, what lies?
    Treasure the hemlock covers—

Skysail of frost, and riding in
    Starlight keen and steep.
But the boy below? What's here is
    Gear in a sea-chest only.
Stowed for a season, then
    Pleasure-bound on the deep.

Dead Child

No hint before? He was dreamy
    Past the ways of children.
Yearning—toward what heaven
    His long lashes curled?
This you imagined after.
    All are rapt, our children.
Gazing out of the window,
    Gazing . . . Out of the world?

Down where the children play,
    The sun casts one less shadow—
Then it's a brighter morning?
    Then it's a broader sun?
No, where one shade faded
    No sun fills the hollow
—Fearful pit, uncovered
    Where the children run.

The Young Ionia

If you could come on the late train for
    The same walk
Or a hushed talk by the fireplace
    When the ash flares
As a heart could (if a heart would) to
    Recall you,
To recall all in a long
    Look, to enwrap you
As it once had when the rain streamed on the
    Fall air,
And we knew, then, it was all wrong,
    It was love lost
And a year lost of the few years we
    Account most—
But the bough blew and the cloud
    Blew and the sky fell
From its rose ledge on the wood's rim to
    The wan brook,
And the clock read to the half-dead
    A profound page
As the cloud broke and the moon spoke and the
    Door shook—

If you could come, and it meant come at the
    Steep price
We regret yet as the debt swells
    In the nighttime
And the *could come, if you could* hum in
    The skull's drum
And the limbs writhe till the bed
    Cries like a hurt thing—
If you could—ah but the moon's dead and the
    Clock's dead.
For we know now: we can give all
    But it won't do,

Not the day's length nor the black strength nor
    The blood's flush.
What we took once for a sure thing,
    For delight's right,
For the clear eve with its wild star in
    The sunset,
We would have back at the old
    Cost, at the old grief
And we beg love for the same pain—for a
    Last chance!
Then the god turns with a low
    Laugh (as the leaves hush)
But the eyes ice and there's no twice: the
    Benign gaze
Upon some woe but on ours no.
    And the leaves rush.

Decline and Fall

We had a city also. Hand in hand
Wandered happy as travellers our own land.
Murmured in turn the hearsay of each stone
Or, where a legend faltered, lived our own.
The far-seen obelisk my father set
(Pinning two roads forever where they met)
Waved us in wandering circles, turned our tread
Where once morass engulfed that passionate head.

Cornice rose in ranges, rose so high
It saw no sky, that forum, but noon sky.
Marble shone like shallows; columns too
Streamed with cool light as rocks in breakers do.

O marble many-colored as reach of thought,
Tones so recollected and so distraught.
Golden: like swimmers when the August shore
Brightens their folklore poses more and more.
Or grey with silver: moon's whirling spell
Over the breathless olives we knew well;
Ivory as shoulders there that summer-dressed
Curve to come shyly naked, then find rest
(The tresses love dishevelled leaning dazed
And grateful). Or the wayward stone that blazed
As cheeks do. Or as eyes half-lowered flare.
Violet as veins are, love knows where.
Fine coral as the shy and wild tonguetip,
Undersea coral, rich as inner lip.

There was a stone to build on!
                       Friezes ran
In strong chorales that where they closed began;
And statues: each a wrung or ringing phrase
In the soul's passionate cadence of her days.

O stone so matched and massive, worked so well,
Who could believe it when the first brick fell?
Who could imagine the unlucky word
Would darken to the worldwide sigh we heard?
How our eyes wrenched together and held fast
Each face tightening to a chalky cast
(So poor a copy of one hour before).
Who could believe the gloom, the funnelled roar
Of cornice falling, forum falling, all
Falling? Or dream it fallen? Not a wall
With eaves to route the rain. The rivers swelled
Till roads groped in lakebottom. Nothing held
Clean edge or corner. Caking, the black flood
Left every luminous room tunnels of mud.
Earth shook: the columns walked, in midair clashed,
And the steep stone exploded as it crashed.

Soon the barbarian swarmed like locusts blown
Between the flood and spasm of our stone.
Grunted to tug their huts and marble sties
Where friezes broke like foam in the blue skies.
Blue noses poked, recoiling as they found
Our young and glad-eyed statues underground;
Singing salvation, the lewd chisel pecks
At boy and girl: one mutilated sex.
All our high moments cheapened—greed and grime
Charred them in rickety stithies to quicklime.

Murderous world. That town that seemed a star
Rose in our soul. And there the ruins are.
We'll not walk there again. Who'd wish to walk
Where the rats gather and grey tourists talk?
Who'd walk there even alive? Or bid his ghost
Trail phosphor on the melancholy coast?

The Lover

The lover of many women in his time
Came to his time: the lap of earth uncloses.
"The true to none?"—with sorrow—"true to none
In the long handsome June of all my roses?"

The lover, faint with pain (death's nuclear flash
Had bared the chambers of his life before him,
Seedy resort hotel with two walls gone,
Beds on all fours and trailing laundry) bore him

Like one assured of sympathy—his ear
So cunning in all cadence of surrender.
His famous smile, the "eternal boy's," began;
His famous wistful shrug. The tone less tender:

"Much from an ancient fate. But not your doom.
Your doom is your conceit of what you are.
Violet-stained, in a white fire of lenses,
Your heart become its will: the cancerous star."

His hell began, a hissing of cold foliage.
Hell too much like Eden. A second glance
Showed in the brush a dozen Eves coquetting—
The country club on nights of the spring dance

Had such mysterious tussle in the shrubbery,
Ruby on velvet hushed, from owl to lark.
But here light hugged the turf, a lunar neon
Of taverns known. The dozen brows were dark.

The enchanted wood exhaling fogs of brandy:
Breasts candlelit, a dream of altars, swim.
Knees like the noble jewels that shaft a chalice.
And cloth of gold about the seraphim.

Fingers beckoning like hands on harpstrings.
Shoulders that ebb consenting. Sweetness choked
His heart in the old vice; he fell sobbing
"Thank God!"—the words sprung jackknives
    in his throat.

Two ankles shone like lotus; he flopped toward them
—Half-blinded seal—and spangled them with kisses
And so kissed up and up in a long whinny
And shivered as he prayed and all delicious.

Kissed to the pulsing throat. Then knew his hell.
A face like a bland egg: no lips to murmur
The summer storm, wet eave, or wishing well.
No breath—perfumed Andalucía yearning.

No human eye: affectionate fern to ring
Woodland pools the ivory bather haunted.
Lovely: hover of heaven, starlit while
The braw boar in the bracken lashed and grunted.

One hope: ears, sensitive orchids of all music—
To drown his grief in comfortable hair.
Fearful, his fingers sought beneath the tresses—
Howled. And a viper of lightning hissed the air.

Polonaise

Dobranoc, kochanie . . .
Pamiętaj o mnie jeszcze trochę . . .

I

The gray-green eyes, Polonia! then the bed
Throned with old trophies of a father dead.
Our star: a plane torn orange from the skies,
Szaro-zielone oczy, gray-green eyes.

Hair: bonfire gold the wind took. Blown amiss—
Half heaven lay blazing in the rain-swept kiss.
Rain taste of salt, *kochanie*? Cheek so cold
Under the sullen splendor, autumn gold?

Lips: in a candle's ardent trance. Or spoke
Rich in a dim significance of smoke.
Wine's lightning, lip to lip, harangued the heart:
Better the soul from body than lips part.

Sun princess, cinnamon-rose: when last we met
The panicky soldier ashen and a-sweat
Hefted his carbine, staring. Shadows close
Over a girl's defiance, cinnamon-rose.

But gardens of the breast, ecstatic still,
No passions empty and no passions fill.
No, though an eagle of Patmos warm her nest
Deep in a dole of roses, flowerbed breast.

II

The flowering breast, Aneczka! still the dead
Vivid as poppies in the armored tread.
The east, a horde unshorn, the shaven west,
Loll in the halftrack hooting, flowery breast.

108

Sun princess, cinnamon-rose: across your cheek
Mark of the darkness speaking when you speak?
Our willow, lovelock in the Vistula, knows
Dark of the moon becomes you, cinnamon-rose.

Hair, ember gold. Pan's tendril at the ear
Dusky with lovesongs of the darkening year.
Trains blunt as thunder, eye almighty, rolled
Over the gala shoulder, autumn gold.

Lips: in a candle's ardent trance. Or wine
Breathing Slavonian starlight in the pine.
At Biskupin—the enchanted cabins—start
Tales of the parted lips, the lips apart.

The gray-green eyes, rain-driven, fade afar.
What journey's end for children of the star?
Courage! He sings—great father—from the skies
Of *szaro-zielone* ever, gray-green eyes.

Parallax at Djebel-Muta

He strolled the desert cliff; tumultuous sunset
Drove a long shadow, phantom, over sands,
Honeycombed long ago—a thunder of granite
Teeters, pitching him down. Numb knees and hands

Gather beneath him; now he droops and rolls
Like a floored boxer his enormous head.
Ten feet above, a jagged edge of sky.
He had a flashlight; gropes, topples instead

Something that rocks like pottery; then the cool
Grooves of chromium fumbled-on in gloom.
Shadows—a black on sepia dance macabre—
Rage in a forty-century-old tomb.

Under an inch of dust, some rags and bone,
Rubble of royalty. The trained eye reads
Skulls of a boy and girl: his lank with fracture,
Hers in a constellation of blue beads.

Cinnamon, cassia, clove, mysterious such
Run from the tippy skull like hourglass sand:
The girl's hair caught close for windy riding,
A ruined cheek lagoons of lotus tanned,

And a whole shoulder by the broken bone
Nearly intact. El Greco lean. Stroked
By fingers shy as a new lover's it
Absently fell apart like ashes poked.

See the man hunched there? See his bleeding knee
Jostle the thirsty bone that, lacquered, dulls
Immediately like blotters? See him breathe
A stuff once sweeter, sounder than all bells?

II

Spring on the desert cliff: a wonder of sunrise
Fair on the chariot sporting Re, his disk
And halo of hooded snakes. Imported horses,
Plumes of flamingo and eye rolling, risk

A four-spoke bumping bronze wheel on the limestone
Lip of the gorge; the riders shout and lean:
She smiling, Nile-green eyes steady, golden
Throat and one shoulder bare. Do you think a queen?

Well his queen. Green pleats belted round his middle,
Shoulders armorial bronze, rein-sailing hand,
With falcon eyes half-shadowed on her, laughing,
Like skiers down and over the dazzling sand

Balancing paired—as for a season flesh
Glories, adoring any dare of soul.
Wide-circling, they rein in: sinew-corded
Burgeoning pillars by a ferny pool

Under two tousselled palms: knotted sandals
Squeal in the padded sand; the lovers' lips
Explore at ease in their lost language, spelt with
Hawks looking hard at you, baboons and ships,

Bee, bittern, king of beasts, the crescent moon—
Flesh and blood alphabet. (Their flesh and blood,
So rich a drift on thornstock of the bone!)
—Even as they kiss, the ghost appeared, midflood

In sunlight, as in mingle of moonlight once
He came inspecting with archaic stare.
A rickety skeleton, gold-circled eyes,
Gold in his teeth, a wide skull without hair;

Left arm leathered to a prank of time;
Right, dry splinters, poking a chrome rod;
Before him buttons floating in air pit-patter
Castanets on his breastbone with each nod.

A breath of air his ruin. Teasing, they
Wheedle him near. Until lips radiant still
Panic the ghost. They, whistling their wild horses,
Sprang and like golden eagles took the hill.

Etruscan Tomb

Tarchna dreams by the distant ocean—
Nobody knows how long a dream.
Sorts of lore
Old when the testy cardinal, blazing,
Ripped his sword from the heinous beam;
Old before:
Look, strange hordes on the bristling shore.
What a humus of tombs! and the ghosts and tokens
Storm like gulls at the furrowing team.

Time out of mind a ledge in a meadow
Nobody saw as heft of hands,
Rainy-grey,
Passed with a glance by the steely Romans
Frowning bigger and better plans—
Now, today,
Look, we have pried stone doors away!
What a burst of birds and frolic of dolphins
Swirling the air like banners and bands!

How they were drunk with hope, these children!
Nobody told them life was dour.
Gloomy tombs?
What, when tombs were salons for living!
Nothing had ended, that was sure.
Laurel blooms,
Look, in the bright, bird-flirting rooms.
What a chuckle of jugs, what crooning copper!
Flowers festooning the furniture!

And treasure catching the breath! in mines why
Nobody struck such eager wealth.
Oh no glow
Of morose ruby, viperous emerald
Here: here's candor and flush of health.
On this stone,

Look! what an outdoor field-fest thrown!
What a bright lense catching the dancers' passion,
Brow's abandon and barefoot stealth.

Horsemen flash on the sundrunk meadow—
Nobody drank so mad a sun,
Shoulders bold.
Eyes in rainbow of golden lashes
Laugh as the high-knee horses run.
Slick as coal,
Look! and the skyblue feyfoot foal!
What a hover of hooves like rippling fingers,
Manes that tangle and thunderous fun.

So friskily ferned and forked an ocean
Nobody sour of spirit knows.
Radiant haze
On the prism cliff and the waves that plop with
Lollop of dolphin springy as bows.
Bathers gaze,
Look, where the innocent fishline strays.
What a plunge from the reef as seabirds scatter!
Bodies simple as flowers unclose.

Though their tongue is a wild conundrum,
Nobody had such lucid hands:
Soothe or hoot,
Confer gently with troubled horses,
Reassure like a loving glance,
Cuddle fruit,
Look, and dazzle the twosome flute!
What a blur of birds! and the wingtip fingers!
Swallowy palms floating over the dance.

That dance! hips like a whisk of fingers;
Nobody had such flings of fun,

Flair as there!
No girl swung on a flank of satin,
None in a shiver of sequin spun
As these wear,
Look! pure limbs and halo of hair.
What a splendor of flesh! as if bones were breathing
Slender a fire as the virgin dawn.

Man's tomb—for the rest what greensick symbols.
Nobody else had lip so live,
Eye so fired.
Others mutter their maybes, pleading
Peacock, phoenix, and yew survive.
Tarchna choired
Look! what the soul itself desired.
What a mumble of skulls and dust from others.
All she sang was *Alive oh alive.*

Tarchna's death is a dive in sunlight.
Nobody knows how deep a dive—
See that sea!
Flung like sun in a seethe of rainbows
Drenched and laughing the dead arise!
Just to be
Look! in so wild bright brash a sea!
What a thunder of surf! and the great locks tossing.
Still she sang *Oh alive and alive.*

Tarchna's dark: in the bronzing twilight
Nobody treks the haunted run.
Broken loam
Scuffing the musk of age and autumn.
Westward, ah the effulgent zone.
Far below
Look! how the carmine harbors glow!
What a thrilling of red like brilliant music,
Like eyelids fast on a rapture of sun.

Roman Letter

inventas aut qui vitam excoluere per artis quique sui memores
alios fecere merendo

What stormy barometers of emotion blown,
Upheaval in heaven, spells of moon and thunder
Over pediments piled to stupefy barbarians!
Odi et amo—girls of the region reaped a
Murderous wind: Rome's ornery as mortality.

Colossal oddments like a hollywood midden,
Lonely location of old superfilms.
How many a neighborhood in double exposure,
Epoch on epoch overthrust, outcropping;
Centuries telescoped like famous trains.

Look at the forum like old molars patched,
Clamps a-grapple and the bogus brick.
Deride if you will—but scuffing the chariot ruts
Of the Sacred Way, such panic of remembrance,
Such brunt of fact, delirium of old triumph
Thuds on the nape of your neck that reason reels.

Except for languor of the world's pretension,
The exhilarance of death and outer space,
Except for the platitudes in aquarelle,
Who'd love the stones of Rome—such brutal spoor
Tracking the verdigris and chalcedony?
The skull of the Colosseum, eaten clean,
(My charming American Daisy, Dublin Maud)
Eroded as old bone, dead as the moon—
What's the right tribute but the eye's aversion?

Remember the Lateran's gilded pugilist,
Thorax swollen like cobra's, cobra head,
Caligula's petted bullyboy?—there's your token.
Where else has propaganda such a pedigree?

It's hard to remember holiness was here
(Though never at home: was here with every horror
Of iron blurting red, of blood-soaked leather)
And left strange traces: a house of God, and aping
Some deified Julian's pool, some de luxe terminal?—
Bragging it's pure: no tourist with bare shoulders;
Bragging boisterously its big physique.

Sanctity's in the cellar yet. Those mines of
Silence and wild conundrum catch the breath.
Saints play at find-the-tomb: all's fabulous
The chisel chinks on here. Reach and rub wonder.

Shaken, reascend to the marble barns—
It's hard to forgive this temple! Best forget,
For Sant' Agnese, San Clemente, Quattro
Coronati, San Prassede's zodiac roof—
All reliquaries, a rapt jeweler's dream:
With God's great eye in jade, his hurricane hair,
His wrestlers and his virgins fierce as trees
Striving and staring where? Beyond. Their passion
Tugs at the world's inertia till it soars.

In Rome, encourage your eye to panorama,
Look far and wide; be chary of close looks
Where highfalutin pilasters weave, performing
St. Vitus' rites. (Cambodia's fevered stone
Is haunted so.) Never mind. We soon accept
As we accept the family bats in belfries,
The taints of a loved face. Come to require them
And wouldn't be without.

                    The face of Rome:
Imperial and autumnal, her remote
Blue eyes half-drowsed with multifarious loves,
Lips stirred voluptuously, the corners still

Triste with atrocities of long ago.
No queen perhaps—an actress all distraction
To men. A face to be milled in mellow gold.

Her color's gold. The color of cut melon
Gives succulence to any lean perspective.
Rome's all air and distance. Where is space
Such an impresario as here? So musical?
With water fluting from shells or plashing its palms
On rataplan troughs or timpani of water;
With air (from high Frascati or the sea's
Black-lava shore Tyrrhenian bathers hail)
A glossy talker in oriels of the laurel
Or tolling the tragic attitude of pines.

Pause on the brink of the Spanish Steps at evening
When the twilight-blooming youth, pale castaways,
Wash to that far-seen crag from every land,
And the schoolgirls swirl in their dirndls to sit
      like lotus;
Or stray on the Pincio redolent of the great
Great dead: look west to the Tiber and Monte Mario,
Where three domes in a row increase and hover
Like balls in a conjurer's palm.

An olio too mauve for candor of beauty,
Too flushed and mournful-eyed, with a trace of tremolo,
Yet here we'd live, and not for the saffron pergolas,
The picnic under the tomb in the Appian meadow—
But for prodigies and a cue or two, the pressure
Of many an atmosphere—all that impregnates
The pine by Egeria's water, the embosoming air.

Florence

The yellow river and the violet hills
Henry James embossed in permanent-black
Jollied a flagging fellow to exuberance.
He saw the angel of Florence: cozy-gold.

Clamber the cobbled ramps in clarion air
To a gravel belvedere breezy and cedary
Lavishing:

      Florence mortised in her hills,
Oxide-rose, a glory of quartz sunning.

Misnomer of blossomy nods, stern fleur-de-lys,
Igneous stone's your heritage and mood.

Listen how testy antiphons come wrangling
From the Palazzo Vecchio, haggard shawm.
Here's varmint-eyed, hard-bit, surly Firenze,
The snarl in the name, no name of blossoms now:
The hanged man's booted somersault from merlons;
Gullet stairs stilettoed bodies bump.

Duck with a sheepish cocktail under its turbulence,
Tourist in sporty shorts. The immense contempt
Of a truncheon torn from thorn, of fangy battlements,
Of a rusty-gold old hauberk-harsh façade
Panics your chattering camera to far corners,
Looms like an old bogy's matterhorn.
Compose its face to serene avatars,
Shrink it to atavism—not a flicker
From the craggy brows that rake Siena still
Through mountainous indigos of execration.

Streets we essayed at every hour: those piquancies
Are graven deep in the brain—the nostril's tingle
At pine-shavings on pavements when the rain

Purpled the somber gorge of Vigna Nuova;
Or flower-banks under the granite mien, a sweetness
Coddled and mocked by dubious ambience:
Boisterous savor of hot herbs from kitchens;
Halls ether-sweet with desuetude; the celery
Reek in lichenous archways, iron-railed
Against such pungency: rankness of time,
Of human life and human love—its mouldering
Packed in the common halidoms we plod.

It's Rome for all cajolery. This Florence
You find in your own heart, if anywhere,
Prizers of wild acridity, sunset-crimson
Rancor of peach too near the rusty pit,
Or thralls of a northern calm, camellia-white
Of swimmers dripping from numb monochrome.

Surely no pendulous angel: cozy-gold.

O candor-of-almond cheek, cool lashes' raillery
Under the lancers' eave one drenching day,
Serene in the great hotel's flurry of foreigners,
Or niched from pitiless snow in San Frediano's
Grot of a door, by the bleak Bar's fluorescence,
Your hair a sowing of stars, oblivious lady—

From over time and the sea my gift, carissima.
Bear it with bantering palm: rough everlastings,
Thistles purple as stelliferous night.

Reflections in Venice

Except for the dowdy splash in back canals,
The lettuce and the lemon bold as brass,
All of that uppity ruckus on the radiant
Bayous dreaming of Byzantium yet,
Who'd ever assent to Venice? Who'd believe?

Men fancy pueblos so in the grand affair
Of a calliope sunset, see them plain
Through thirst over the witty sand's delirium.
Men have whimsies—but indulge them in marble?
Throw a bold roof on hallucination?
"Venice unseats the reason." Rather say
Reason became a delicate madman, chortled
Over preposterous blueprints. And approved them.
The daily bread's absurdity. What can never
Exist (for all of the bees in reason's bonnet)
You stub your toe on. The best leather scuffs.

Because the incredible's hourly and of course,
What takes the breath is wonder of banality:
The gondolier's shovelling shoulder, quirky wrist
(His long stroke like a billow tripped on shale)
Sculling not lovers but a bathtub, rags,
Mattresses, cabbage, or a coop with cacklers;
While over his sousing route one traffic light,
Alice's tabby—look!—appearing, disapp—

A straight line here?—anathema! Sobersided
Cities behave like waffles. Venice no.
Her gold palazzi ripple like theater curtains
When a door opens offstage on reality.
That Venice in the water, upside-down,
Is nearly as sound, as practical to live in.

Her skin: a great sea-creature hauled ashore,
Rind, hackle, hide and dewlap beached and fading

Under that glare from splendor of the depths
To grey of shale and pebble, of kelp sunning.

Watch how the walkers bob like kangaroo
Over the little bridges (pretty rickrack:
Wickets for the ancient sea disporting).
Streets are a crinkum-crankum, lithographed
Gameboard of Advance Three or Back to Start,
Left in a night of rain to bleach and frizzle.

What's for a prize? Ca' d'Oro: faded seine,
Her grey and coral plaited to catch time.
Opposite, in the fishmart, brooms of bracken
Scuffle the onion, orange-paper, sage.

What's for a prize? San Marco, malapert
To Parthenon-doting eyes: extravagant baggage!

A Cretan dancer on back somersault
Arching breast-up on ivory heel and finger.

At sunset, like a Valentine afire
That nick of time before it sags and blackens.

Tawny and sweet within, dark honeycomb
Of buckwheat shuffled with bright combs of clover.

Above, the dome's old glow—an artist's bowl
Where grime of gold was puddled till it crusted,
Left in a cupboard under cellar stairs
—A cat's eye in a jungle!—among cobwebs.

Hers is a floor, no, not to walk—to wade:
Lurching like sandbars under surf. Our weight
Thrills in the pitch and drag of seafloors drained,
The flora charmed, the osprey flat as fossils.

And the great souls that people the dark mountain!
Massing in fabulous funnies, fey charade.

Their gestures few as semaphores know poses.

Woe's a contusion, joy a vivid gash
On faces scored like boxers': chuck-full
Of rough conviction, nuggets in a gunny sack.

Where these parade, in stalagmite for toga,
The stone's alive: four-footed homes, pagodas
Shamble on pillar shank like headless pets.
All's neighborly: the houses men step out of
Crouch at their heel and sit there till commanded,
Handy as stools. The fishermen ease rumps
Into the cockleshells they're broader than.
All as it should be. These were made for mortals.

As mortals were for God. Why should great spirits
Fuss and truckle to pernickety blubber?
They've better things to con than right anatomy—
Eyes spellbound on the languorous green prince
Draped zigzag on his crisscross; on the angels
Gawky as new-hatched eagles from the shell;
On the great father's caving face of doom,
Beard like a snowslide in the Pyrenees.

Leaving the trance of northern night, go blinking
Into a blizzard of pigeons. Puzzle on it:
Venice, a shopworn rainbow. Maybe. But
In time's kaleidoscope what spunkier sparkle
As the great kingdoms pyramid and slip?
If man must have a single den, be denizen,
Venice would do. As well as Waffleopolis,
Suburbia's forty winks, or Little Wotting.

She'll set the wits a-tintinnabulating!

Restorative music in our time. And sovereign
For many a subtle canker. If it's granted
Our grief is of the heart or of the reason,
Settle in Venice, traveller—lose both.

A Frieze of Cupids

Qui su l'arida schiena
Del formidabil monte
Sterminator Vesevo . . .

Pompeii: the seedy vendors
Ruffle and palm their books
Under the tourists'
Stirred or averted looks,

On spying limbs in love here
Long centuries ago.
How, and how much? The tourists
Pay furtively to know.

Visions mauve and tender.
Scenes queasily sad:
The grey grit laid forever
Whatever bloom they had.

Lava composed their spirit.
Withered the wing of pride.
The mountain lapped these lovers
In a long side-by-side.

That incest-ridden mumbler
Heard the infernos call—
His lewd effusion dooming
The children one and all.

Originated in a Chorus of Satyrs

Had eager Eve for whose sweet will we languish,
Had Adam culled the garden as he should,
What of the great tale then: stone torso of anguish
Lost for the soft samoas of the wood?
Which of the three hurled *mawkish* at the florid
Dead-end of time? God's proxy manned to act?
Eve pondering palm on thigh? The Andean forehead
Blazing in clouds and lightning: *false to fact?*

Whose notion to explode the halcyon deadlock,
Dunging the garden with felicitous sin?
Harrow the native clay? Go clean to bedrock?
Which of the three hailed scathing vision in
When the eighth day made history?

                                    Pity and dread
Blazon like haloes the great blinded head.

Ancient of Days

Spellbound as lunar buttes, the terrible past
Because it lies before me chills the bone.
In Knossos at high noon I mooned, dreamfast
On girls cartwheeling in sunflowers over the stone,
Schist or selenite. Or heard of worse:
Tar cocoons in earth the effendis sight
And syphoning in hot wax, tease back to birth
Ecce-homo's of lip-withering night.

Unless the opposable thumb (with crown and crozier:
Not pottering now in fields of Pleistocene)
Prove to our joy the pearly world's disposer
And not time's by-blow, as sucked craniums mean:—
Souls' saturnalia then! the moon's great gong
Enthralling the fairy pintos of the dawn!

And a Fortune in Olive Oil

Sweeten the moody world, Milesian waters,
Sparkle on Ur, on Lagash where it lies;
Drenching in dew the fertile crescent, scatter
The rosegold rumps babooning in the skies.
Flow to the squatting mother, nipples rigid,
Pupils of milkglass from the idiot sun,
Nursing her private Nile—over the turgid
Cats of the sand let freshets bubble and run

Rafting the first man ever to stand upright,
Ever through aqueous humor view the world,
Even its pyramids!—who (dared their true height)
Eyed the wide shadow on dominions hurled,
Bestriding his own: huffed gilas when he spoke
Ruptured like puffballs in irascible smoke.

Affair at the Fork

The gods leaned forward at his bursting forth
Thick-booted out of Corinth, hating the business,
Hellbent for anywhere else. Rampaging north
(His face an icon of dust from the dim isthmus)
He clashed with foreigners where ruts contorted,
Glorying, "Room for the king of Corinth's son!"
High in the cart, an apparition snorted
And ground the hub on his leg—the sensitive one.

Damnation! Blind with pain, his temples pealing,
He wrestled the gauntface down, brow stunning brow,
Rolled savage among slaves, till passion cooling
Crooned for him tunes of decent headway now.
The gods sank back enchanted: flattering bell!
When had the fractious planet run so well?

Calliope to Clio

μῆνιν ἄειδε, θεά, Πηληϊάδεω Ἀχιλῆος
οὐλομένην, ἣ μυρί' Ἀχαιοῖς ἄλγε' ἔθηκε . . .

The red wrath of Achilles—cope with that,
Muse, if you dare. Look doting on disaster:
Heroes dumped arsy-versy in hades' grot,
Lurid as lava pattering faster faster.
Flesh given to dogs—what bloomed in a queen's eye
Angry elastic snaggled in the fang;
And what the soaked crows spatter as they fly;
All this. Last, how the oxhorn lamina rang

As the lounging god (in profile to display
Better the measured nose, serene lip curling),
Called nonchalantly his targets, and let fly
With whinny of pleasure arrows cool as sterling.
That statue of him, though broken: the fine eye
Flicks unconcerned—why not?—the unnerving sky.

Ishtar

Two ordinary people, nextdoor neighbors—
Surely nothing for legend in these two:
He swishing in mint (his only labors),
Whirring matched irons over clover and dew.
And she for parties: the gold lighter poises
Shy in her fingers, an assyrian bird.
A downward smile, gilt sandals flexing. Voices
Curl in a pillowy corner, half unheard.

That night, the bedlamp fitful in her room;
Panes staring black and anxious. A race
Of lightning (thunder held, amassing doom)
Quivered long drenching seconds on each face.

Sweet firebird, fly away; fade, golden shoe.
Wait long and long, bright irons, for the dew.

A Pretty Device of the Fathers

A dagger (whose bone haft the iceberg locks)
Prime diamond in the nights of polar cold:
Sharpened by shamans haloed in white fox,
Their faces bland (obols of scythian gold)—
Butt fused in ice: the uncanny tool upstanding
Whetted so fine it sang in the least wind,
A glamor the grey lopers took to haunting,
Each eye a prickle of fire: wolves winter-thinned

Pad furry-eyed, tongues hankering for that bangle
(Bobbing like censers to the illustrious vault):
One runs a tongue along the edge: a tingle
Teases him, warm and sticky, thrilling of salt.
Delirious attar of life! The ecstatic glare
Glues them in furry carnage, sweet fangs bare.

Natione non Moribus

(1265–1321)

. . . shrug off the world (as churning boys
    leather head tucked, shake tacklers and reel free)
    forgetting, just like that, the ingenious toys,
red hearts and yellow hair, the unstable quay,
    that tedium and Te Deum of our days,
    and with a mind clean as amnesia see:
the wanderer's double world, where intermaze
    (gold comb in gypsy hair) the event and vision:
    the Roman mouth its dark as copper phrase
long under dust, imperious with decision;
    woods hoarse and murky as unloading of coal,
    bitch-eyed libido in light air's derision—
        then, from the deck of planets as they roll
        to breathe that air! And breathless . . . at the Pole . . .

The Academy Disporting

In love with shadows all our days,
Creepers shunning dark and bright:
The dutiful, who troop to gaze
On friendship's long-exhausted rite;
To fob and shuffle palm to palm
Coppers of accustomed thought:
Decades have tested all we say;
And we lope roguish, as they taught.

Beneath the mistletoe will drift
Kisses the flat "punch" half warms.
Wan mirage of kisses. No
Likelihood of thunderstorms.
Compilers would look far to find
Milder perversities of lust.
There is no ruby in this ash:
Kisses that half stir the dust.

White shoulders we would press today—
Time is a great page torn between!
We nibble polite watercress
Fresher than memory, more green
Than Junes which gloated-over here
Would blast the many-eyebrowed room,
Alarming almost to its feet
The tableau stable as a tomb.

From where the soul with level look
Is hinting its contempt too well,
We flee—who cannot be alone—
Like bats poured panicky from hell.
From where the eye we dare not meet
Burns ruby in immortal bronze,
We break and run like giggling kids—
Ecstatic if a portal clangs.

Is there no lightning in the land
To show us, bitter black and white,
The car, the cottage, and the dune,
The hound a-howling all that night,
And where the imprudent, hand in hand,
Sway naked in immortal surf?
What vision haunts the summer land?
What wound is closing in the turf?

Shrimp on little picks impaled
Lie naked to the decent eye,
Grey frost their bed. Our fingers lift,
Insert them goggling, and put by—
Quashing a thunder in the soul
That rages to make all things right:
In love with shadows all our days,
Creepers shunning dark and bright.

Isaiah's Coal

what more can man desire?

Always, he woke in those days
With a sense of treasure,
His heart a gayer glow
Than his window grand with sun,
As a child, its mind all whirring
With green and hollied pleasure
Wakes in a haze of *Christmas!*
The season of secrets done.

Or as one on country linen
Wakes with a start one morning—
Then on comfort snugger than pillows
Floats: July at the lake.
Or has married a golden girl
And can hardly believe, but turning
Sees blossom for him that very face
Worshipping cameras take.

Toy trains whirr perky on
Till springs contort beneath;
The middle-age rower slumps
Like a sack—indignant seizure!
Late editions wail
Screen Star in Mystery Death—
Yet in those same days
He woke with a sense of treasure.

Knowing: my love is safe
Though the Rockies plunge like water,
Though surf like a wildfire rage
And omens roam the sky;
Though limbs of the swimmer laze
Pale where the seaweed caught her,
Nothing can touch my love
As dangerous time goes by.

Last Judgment

When we are ranged on the great plain of
    flabbergasting death,
Feeding (for our lungs hang slack) on air not drawn
    with breath,
And see, for many miles around, our Easter Island lie,
The gaping dumbshow of our shame, in footlights
    from the sky:
How many a scene long out of mind in rooms we
    barely knew,
Punch amok or Judy lewd, lit fuchsia-red or blue,
And see our working face in each and sway a
    moment numb—
Then save us from our rage Yourself; let lightning
    cry our doom!
Having such motive for their hate, each knowing
    what it knows—
We know our terrible hearts too well to trust our
    luck with those.

De Fide

Do you believe in Him? you ask. Safer to say No,
Since what I'd be admitting could be a death of snow,
Some hatchet whacks on an old log where pigmies
    slit the skin,
A Moses-beard, tremendous crag, or formulas of wind.
To these and maybe yours, it's No. But for another
    there—
You'd wonder, when I fill my lungs: Do you
    believe in air?

Old River Road

One party of that season. Evening journals
Whirred to their perch oblivious of doom.
The two reposed their coats. Flanked on a sofa
Sat innocent of the other. Chaffed the room

Till hands by chance encountering in cashews
(Roaming a moment from their tutor eyes)
Touched. And a current flowed. The two were dazzled:
Their hands! to play such lightning from the skies

As rocked impeccable homes to their foundation,
Loosened a promise and shook plaster down,
Baited that pack, the chaste uncharitable
Tongues till they bred contagion about town.

What matter tongues? What matter to the blinding
Mask of agony what the chorus bays?
Touched. And he doffed the satin visor: met her
Delft and undecipherable gaze

Much like the morning spangled in his lashes.
What of the brow's sereneness? Or the hair
Cool and amused, remembering crowns her fervor
Burned to the smoky gold of autumn air?

What of her gaze the gala night deciphered
Pondering mottoes of the barbarous dart?
Thanks to the ash on his lapel consulted
And the false candor of a sinking heart?

Eyes in the other's gloried like plumes tossing
That more and more sang *morituri* plain.
So gladiators in their clanking bonnet
Planting their sandals on the arrogant stain,

Eyes like coals in a great brazier glowing
Around and round the impending thousands scan,
Seizing the noon for omen! Hola, lobo!
Bloat on the rich disaster if you can.

II

Both overfrank. In part to trip suspicion,
Part for that dragging mantle, laissez-faire,
Part for the gin, like sacred lamps attended,
They feigned embrace. A spectacle, the pair.

Anon, his tail between his legs, discretion
Deserted these, to mutter among drunks.
A spectacle of some concern to husbands,
Bumbling men unbudgeable as trunks;

Of some concern to keepers of the linen,
Bleak with the blue mondays of the past.
Their keys a-jangle: moon-resistant, May-proof.
Oh that candor were as season-fast!

Laocoön, you would have winked to see them.
Laocoön, out Lackawanna way?
Wrapped in their own bright spirals of endearment
And much aspersed by yodellers. Break of day

Found them the worse for friendly wear: a huddle
Baroque and dowdy, on a jumble of knees.
A hoyden skirt the merciful amended.
The indecent dead are howling rites like these.

Her face a sleepy flower. A child's in fever.
Once in a strange forest long ago
The birds, a shimmer of cocktail hues, came loosing
Leaves where the lost children slept below

As mist impearled the conifers. The matted
Lashes of both the tears enchanted fast.
Delicate: a rare flying thing, its lacy
Wings in the gold collodion of the past.

The tears were hard to pardon. Much-forgiving
Spouses protested water into wine.
But tears are tears. The two had each a reason:
Early morning, and the day's decline.

III

Brave words at first: the night of nine auroras
Rooting in curious forms of fern and wood
Chanced on a thing of earth the astonished lovers
Had scrupled to imagine if they could.

Angels beckoning Adam to the garden
Shaped with their fingers, flaming, what they meant:
Fuddled the lost lovers with indulgence
No will of theirs had ventured to invent.

They spurned the bogus bloom, cadaverous waxes,
Gathering what abounded and no more.
Stung with no iron glove the face of heaven,
Come to this pretty pass at heaven's door.

But candors flashed, admissible in marble;
Marble darkened with considerate blood;
Blood was a raging main; the embattled galleon
Toppled doubloons and javelins in the flood

As the foam scrolled: Finale. A quick curtain.
Gawky, the room and furniture trooped in.
They sagged in their embrace, straitjackets giving;
Human heads a-loll with dingy grin.

Breath on the lip, so debonaire a spender
It left the lung no penny of its own,
Shrunk. They felt the hollow in those gaudy
Breasts that festoon the musty coops of bone.

The hollow between heartbeats; looming lobo
Hard on the heels of valor in the snow.
—What of the bright balloon, heaven's effervescence?
Trodden on fairgrounds when the wagons go

To the next town, indifferent, leaving rutted
Yesterday's joy, the fields of pleasure torn.
Where the white queens performing—swans of heaven!
Swooned on their buoyant pole. Like twins unborn

The lovers huddle. Glittering wings that weave
Robes of the forest for our sons and daughters,
Lap them in love, who shrivel as they wait
Numbly, a spirit moving on the waters.

IV

We are that key the fugitive finger leaves
As soaring gloria stumbles and recovers;
Chords for the Astra Khan roll kansas-black
Packing a violet fire for hidebound lovers.

Lightning: a lifeline between two and heaven
(September's not more pendulous on its stem).
Give the mad gleeman scope; the tarns of Auber
Foster a lotus moon for even them.

We knew one night the neighborhood was shaken,
Explosions underground: till two and two
The sleepers in their crazyquilt, leaves bleaching,
Mushroomed up. As broken springs would do.

Jack in his proper box. But in the pulpit?
Candor in crow or lobo, duck and drake?
An old wives' tale, remember? And what draughtsman
Caught for his rule the wrist-enchaining snake?

But even these! Her footfall shy and naked
Full on the arrogant stain as javelins rang:
A nine-days' leer to shoeclerks who live crouching,
Immaculate dentists catering to fangs.

These meant a noble fitt, but tripped on Aleph
Crooked as rails where ploughing trains collide.
And saw too much in a wrong season. Others
Suffer their trouble late, as saucers ride

Harrowing sky. The Angel of Death in heaven
(Lunatic sunrise in the dead of night)
Sows in our fallow face the ash of roses.
Dust in the eye's a charm for seeing right.

Conclusion

legato con amore in un volume ciò che per l'universo si squaderna . . .

If what began (look far and wide) will end:
This lava globe huddle and freeze, its core
Brittle with cold, or pulled too near its friend
Pop once like one gun in a long-drawn war,
And the stars sputter one by one, the night
So empty judging *empty*'s out of date
(Space and time gone), then only, height on height,
Mind that impelled those currents and that freight,
Mind that after five days (see those days!
Regions all tropic one day, one all ice!)
Whistled man from the sea-moss, saw him raise
The blundering forepaw, blink from shaggy eyes—
If image, likeness in the ox-yoke brow
Long out of focus, focused mind to Mind—
Ah what unspeakable two and two allows
That silence huddle and all eyes go blind?
Our ups and downs—there! that remembered makes
Memory which is the single mind. How sweet
Carmine stars of the maple fumed in rakes
At 1350 such and such a street.
A thing to keep in mind. Yes and keep yet
When the vile essence violescence lies.
Once in winter by the richening sill
Quiet, the fireplace tiny in our eyes—
I mention this; there's more. The Almighty will
Aeons late stumble on it with surprise.

OF FLESH AND BONE

1967

. . . *is* there more? More than Love and
Death? Then tell me its name!

—Emily Dickinson

Few Things to Say

It's true, we write so little. Years between
Words in this, that, or the other magazine.
Few things to say—two maybe. Girls, know why?
You craze the air with pleasure. And you die.

Days of Our Years

It's brief and bright, dear children; bright and brief.
Delight's the lightning; the long thunder's grief.

At Dawn

"Living!" I grieved. "Each heartbeat, touch-and-go."
Sleepy, you touch and grin: "What touches, though!"

Love

"For when we have blamed the wind, we can
    blame love."
Who'd blame the mindless wind? Sleepers that start
In fear when the ceilings heave like seas above?
Girls with their shattered dresden in the heart?

Parting

"We met in error. If too close,
　　Regrets. And I'm away.
Yesterday was easy come;
　　Easy go, today.
Forget the way we burned, we two,
　　That pain on either part.
Forget we fell convulsed as one."

　　Said knifeblade to the heart.

Contemplation

"I'm Mark's alone!" you swore. Given cause to
　　doubt you,
I think less of you, dear. But more about you.

Anacreon's Answer

"No sense of age? These white hairs on your head,
You take this gold and pink thing to your bed?"
　　　　Of age? For men, two sorts alone are doled:
　　　　The dead years. The alive years, white or gold.
　　　　I and the pink thing are alive-years-old.

Protestation

"You say so, but will you be faithful? You men!"
But dear, I've been faithful again and again!

Epitaph for a Light Lady

Once, lovely Chloe here asleep in clay
Warmed with warm flesh whatever place she lay.
And now so long abed, yet cold as stone?
And—so unlike our Chloe—sleep alone?

With Fingering Hand
Goethe, *Römische Elegien*, 5, 16

Ten thousand cigarettes from now,
   As many drinks away,
I may forget—"O honey, hush!
   Let sleeping lovers lay."
Let sleeping lovers *lie*, my dear.
   "I know as well as you.
But here's a love that's out for rhyme.
   Can't even that be true?"

Avant-garde

"A dead tradition! Hollow shell!
Outworn, outmoded—time it fell.
Let's make it new. Rebel! Rebel!"
Said cancer-cell to cancer-cell.

Visiting Poet

"The famous bard, he comes! The vision nears!"
Now heaven protect your booze. Your wife. Your ears.

Transplant

When I've outlived three plastic hearts, or four,
Another's kidneys, corneas (*beep!*), with more
Unmentionable rubber, nylon, such—
And when (*beep!*) in a steel drawer (DO NOT TOUCH!),
Mere brain cells in a saline wash, I thrive
With thousands, taped to quaver out, "Alive!"—
God grant that steel two wee (*beep!*) eyes of glass
To glitter wicked when the nurses pass.

View from Moon

Once on the gritty moon (burnt earth hung far
In the black, rhinestone sky—lopsided star),
Two gadgets, with great fishbowls for a head,
Feet clubbed, hips loaded, shoulders bent. She said,
"Fantasies haunt me. A green garden. Two
Lovers aglow in flesh. The pools so blue!"
He whirrs with masculine pity, "Can't forget
Old superstitions? The earth-legend yet?"

Philosopher

He scowled at the barometer: "Will it rain?"
None heard, with all that pattering on the pane.

Minotaur

Sweet flesh was shipped the bull-man once to eat.
You think it's changed, you children on the street?
Go home and pack. Tomorrow, off for Crete.

Embroidery at Bayeux

Men fought with axes, panting, nose to nose.
Women with pretty stitches pictured those.
The severed head lies beaming, "I'm a rose!"

Sophomore

Last year I'd tease, "So beautiful! So dumb?"
She'd laugh "I guess," and let the tears half come.
"Confuse such easy lines?" "I tried and tried!"
"Julie, you moon at school. All dreamy-eyed!"
     So last year. Now, as girls lie on the sand
     In summer, hair flung over cheek on hand,
     She—by the curb, in pink of flares. Poor head,
     Lost in your dreams? Confuse *Early to bed?*

On the One Theme Still

In traffic shuddering as it shied too near
That tumble of lovelocks at the silent ear,
She lay, outstretched as if for pleasure, more
Languid than any girl on any shore.
Love taught the pose. *Such cronies, love and death?*
Old bosom friends. If differing, by a breath.

Love and Death

And yet a kiss (like blubber)'d blur and slip,
Without the assuring skull beneath the lip.

The Visit

I loved a girl: She died. I stood here, so;
Stared at the something strangers put below.
Again I stand a moment. Not to stay.
Evenings she'd tease, "Don't wait if I'm away."

Lovers

And here the two by the one grievance haunted
Lie in the dark. But not the dark they wanted.

Perfect Rhyme

Life, that struck up his cocky tune with *breath,*
Finds, to conclude in music, only *death.*

THE KISS: A JAMBALAYA

1982

Béseme de besos de su boca, porque buenos tus amores más que el vino.
—Fray Luis de León, *Exposición del Cantar de Cantares*

The Observatory Ode
Harvard, June 1978

I

The Universe:
We'd like to understand,
But any piece, in the palm, gets out of hand,
Any stick, any stone,
—How mica burns!—or worse,
Any star we catch in pans of glass,
Sift to a twinkle the vast nuclear zone,
Lava-red, polar-blue,
Apple-gold (noon our childhood knew),
Colors that through the prism, like dawn through Gothic, pass,
Or in foundries sulk among grots and gnomes, in glare of zinc or brass.
Would Palomar's flashy cannon say? Would you,
Old hourglass, galaxy of sand,
You, the black hole where Newton likes to stand?

II

Once on this day,
Our Victorian renaissance-man,
Percival Lowell—having done Japan,
And soon to be seen
Doing over all heaven his way—
Spoke poems here. (These cheeks, a mite
Primped by the laurel leaves' symbolical green,
Should glow like the flustered beet
To scuff, in his mighty shoes, these feet.)
He walked high ground, each long cold Arizona night,
Grandeurs he'd jot: put folk on Mars, but guessed a planet right,
Scribbling dark sums and ciphers at white heat
For his Pluto, lost. Till—there it swam!
Swank, with his own P L for monogram.

III

Just down the way
The Observatory. And girls
Attending, with lint of starlight in their curls,
To lens, 'scope, rule.
Sewing bee, you could say:
They stitch high heaven together here,
Save scraps of the midnight sky. Compile, poll, pool.
One, matching star with star,
Learns that *how bright* can mean *how far.*
That widens the galaxies! Each spiraling chandelier
In three-dimensional glamour hangs; old flat nights disappear.
Desk-bound, they explore the immensities. Who are
These women that, dazed at dusk, arise?
—No Helen with so much heaven in her eyes.

IV

With what good night
Did the strange women leave?
What did the feverish planet-man achieve?
A myth for the sky:
All black. Then a haze of light,
A will-o'-the-wisp, hints *time* and *place.*
Whirling, the haze turned fireball, and let fly
Streamers of bright debris,
The makings of our land and sea.
Great rafts of matter crash, their turbulence a base
For furnaces of nuclear fire that blast out slag in space.
Primal pollution, dust and soot, hurl free
Lead, gold—all that. Heaven's gaudy trash.
This world—with our joy in June—is a drift of ash.

V

That fire in the sky
On the Glorious Fourth, come dark,
Acts "Birth of the Universe" out, in Playland Park.
Then a trace of ash
In the moon. Suppose we try
—Now only suppose—to catch in a jar
That palmful of dust, on bunsens burn till it flash,
Could we, from that gas aglow,
Construct the eventful world we know,
Or a toy of it, in the palm? Yet our world came so: we are
Debris of a curdled turbulence, and dust of a dying star
—The children of nuclear fall-out long ago.
No wonder if late world news agree
With Eve there's a creepy varmint in the Tree.

VI

The Universe:
. . . *Such stuff as dreams are made on* . . .
Yet stuff to thump, to call a spade a spade on.
No myth—Bantu,
Kurt, Urdu, Finnish, Erse—
Had for the heaven such hankering
As ours, that made new eyes for seeing true.
For seeing what we are:
Sun-bathers of a nuclear star,
Scuffing through curly quarks—mere fact a merry thing!
Then let's, with the girls and good P. L., sing carols in a ring!
Caution: combustible myth, though. Near and far
The core's aglow. No heat like this,
No heat like science and poetry when they kiss.

Cardiological

Ten heartbeats back our lips were touching. Ten?
Sixteen now, call it. Twenty-something. Truth
Can't manage this, can't get the hang of numbers.
Forty, and counting . . .

As the seas might drive,
Surge over surge, survivors from a raft
Their fingertips had touched once.

Stop that surge?
Stop, you can say to every clock but one
—Steeple-clock, travel-clock, cuckoo-clock—all but one:
The heart, with its red-jeweled steady movement, moves
This moment, this now, this all-our-life away,
Earth, with its birds and steeples, all away.

The prouder, the more impulsive, the more it takes.

Worse: our good moments, song, the mug swung high,
Gaze brimming gaze, the very clod upsoaring,
Joy at its most convulsive—even in dream—
Sting, like a lash, the stumbling heart—stampeding
With *more! yet more!* its irreversible beat.

Tide Turning

Through salt marsh, grassy channel where the shark's
A rumor—lean, alongside—rides our boat;
Four of us off with picnic-things and wine.
Past tufty clutters of the mud called *pluff,*
Sun on the ocean tingles like a kiss.
About the fourth hour of the falling tide.

The six-hour-falling, six-hour-rising tide
Turns heron-haunts to alleys for the shark.
Tide-waters kiss and loosen; loosen, kiss.
Black-hooded terns blurt kazoo-talk—our boat
Now in midchannel and now rounding pluff.
Lolling, we eye the mud-tufts. Eye the wine.

The Atlantic, off there, dazzles. Who said wine-
Dark sea? Not this sea. Not at noon. The tide
Runs gold as chablis over sumps of pluff.
Too shallow here for lurkings of the shark,
His nose-cone, grin unsmiling. *Cr-ush!* the boat
Shocks, shudders—grounded. An abrupt tough kiss.

Our outboard's dug a mud-trough. Call that *kiss?*
Bronze knee bruised. A fair ankle gashed. With "wine-
Dark blood" a bard's on target here. The boat
Swivels, propeller in a pit, as tide
Withdraws in puddles round us—shows the shark-
Grey fin, grey flank, grey broadening humps of pluff.

Fingers that trailed in water, fume in pluff.
Wrist-deep, they learn how octopuses kiss.
Then—shark fins? No. Three dolphins there—*shhh!*—arc
Coquettish. As on TV. Cup of wine
To you, slaphappy sidekicks! with the tide's
Last hour a mudflat draining round the boat.

The hourglass turns. Look, tricklings toward the boat.
The first hour, poky, picks away at pluff.
The second, though, swirls currents. Then the tide's
Third, fourth—abundance! the great ocean's kiss.
The last two slacken. So? We're free, for wine
And gaudier mathematics. Toast the shark,

Good shark, a no-show. Glory floats our boat.
We, with the wine remaining—done with pluff—
Carouse on the affluent kisses of the tide.

Postcard from Minnesota

Last night I scrawled on a postcard *Love and Kisses*
In their curlicues: runes and doodles.
Now I ruminate: *kiss.* What it meant?

    Here watching for dawn by a lake in Minnesota
    On a deck
    Of the barn-red lodge, at the hour it's delicious
        shivering:
    All of the east expectant
                —holding—
                          gorgeous,
    Like curtains hung for a jubilee of sultans.
    The many-a-mile-wide water waits, all nods, a
    Decal of the airy hues there—hues, not colors—
    Decal of their silk on graininess of sailcloth.
    The long lake-levels
    Pull southward, crinkling a little, as if on rollers.
    Over the frosty glitter
    Some diving ducks, offshore, rump-up go under;
    Some Canada geese, wings pumping, beaks directional,
    Are skimming the wild-rice patch, the blowing
        lake-grass.

    Above, just over the jigsaw ridge of jack pine
    The heron, its black
    Pick javelin-sharp, its black wings jagged as hemlock,
    Black shin-rack hanging,
    Flaps out of Jurassic canyons to this morning.

What a kiss is for, I was wondering. All's a part of it.
The dawn wind over the fin-rich water's part of it.

    Wind cool, wind husky with skunk—over fern,
        through cedar—
    On the lake does a dusky shuffle now. Like echoes
    Of the loon, last night, on the full moon's zigzag
        catwalk.

And here, by the open porch-rail,
With a bowl of the old-rose raspberries, nestled
    yesterday
In your blue bandanna
        (Hard-lacquered
        Blackberries you plunk in a pail, but these you
            nestle),
                        just yesterday, after the downpour,
Sun scorching our skin, leaves chill, with a rinse of
    raindrops.

Wild berries. Their flesh a honeycomb, hexagonal,
Curled in on themselves like the universe,
    outside-inside.
A Moebius trick—we can taste it.
Now a-bob on a level of cream, as embossed on vellum.
I glaze them in gilt with a swirl of our buckwheat honey
Trailed from a spoon,
Then sway it to spell out *love*
In script like the dawn's own gold on the medieval
Initial *O* of the bowl, its rose and ivory
—With a fine enough line you twirl *e* before *l* goes
    under.
But to bobble them, half afloat!
                        and to topple them over
The spoon-rim (its cozy oval
Drawn snug in the lips' twin curve), to fumble them
Up, and to mull on the tongue
                        those chummy, tumbling—

Inside them, a tickle of honey the tongue-tip thrills on—

And to crush, crush up lusher the pulp, red cells a fission
Of tiny electrical tingles,
A chain reaction—synaptic, galactic—no difference—

And to feel how they tease, a seed in the teeth, wedged
   testy,
Just a hint of cantankerous earth, old rancor's relish—!

                    ". . . a world in a grain of sand . . ."

And to sense, in the flesh of things, in their flow, a
   beyondness,
Power poured as from outer space—!

The kiss:
I suppose it meant something like this?
Like sharing a world?
                    Not everyone's maybe.
                              Yours . . .

Slapstick I

Meditation for the Morning: Linguistics and the Kiss

> . . . *illo purpureo ore suaviata* . . .
> —Catullus, XLV

Love and Kisses we write, on the backs of our Tru-Kolor
   Fotos.
Now I think about *kiss.*
Ugly word in the mouth, with its—ouch!—little dental-pick *k;*
Its vowel with no music at all, and that snake-hiss of *s*'s.

And the cock-a-snook rhymes it comes schlepping. But
   better not think.
Kiss is cousin to *cuss,* a good word: *cuss* can cuss, but *kiss*
   kiss?
Not a word the lips linger on lovingly,
Although meant to mean: lingering lips.

Φίλημα's a lovemaking word now: your own, Aphrodite.
You can throw yourself too, *con amore* and how, into *bacio.*
Young Catullus imported that word,
Put the kibosh on *osculum*
Bringing *basium* down from Verona—known later for lovers.

Basium—that's from *sua* [*v/b*]*ium* (sweet):
Suabium inside out, as the lips wish to be in a kiss.

There's that word again—*kiss!*
Northern Puritans spat that flat *kiss.*
Couldn't open their mouths in the cold?
So no full-mouth affection?

Well, we're stuck with the word.
                  How get rid of it?
                      How kiss it off?

Dawn Song

. . . to flute the pneuma . . .

Dearest, sleep. Bright night is gone.
Sleep away the dark of dawn.
  It's cold water now for drinking,
  Lids in the cold mirror blinking:

Face of clay, old trashy head.
Dearest, what of what you said?
  Such a one as this before me—
  Such, the midnight kisses swore me?

You said I was—thus and so.
You said—a bit more, you know.
  Mostly, high baroque was spoken;
  Mirror—chill of wind chimes—broken.

Never ivy twined so tight,
Held sprung alabaster right.
  Never, so in ivy sighing,
  At a stand were birth and dying.

Once another, great books say,
Made me out of the cold clay;
  Meant the dust I wear for glory—
  But of course, of course! *Our* story:

Lo, I lay cold clay alone
Till your hand sprung flesh and bone.
  Easter then: the world's untombing;
  Even lunar ash ablooming.

(Such entrusting, yours to me!
Hide your eye: the enchanted tree
  Twined with lightning Eve our mother!
  Such entrusting of each other!)

Love whose joy is second cause,
Cantilevering great laws
    On the porphyry corbel, knew you;
    Laughed to flute the pneuma through you:

"Body floral and velour,
Stir the dullard. Mull amour
    Of your honey, sun, or fertile
    Moon of melon, cotes of myrtle."

What he so projected, you
Took in hand, dear, and saw through.
    He in fangy strata laid me,
    Till you to his image made me.

Image: in the dismal sink,
Skinny, shivering, I blink.
    Back to the deep bed go weaving,
    Which—the glass or you?—believing?

Glass is glass. No inwit there
Stunned the emblazoned dove in air.
    What if shiny mirror shame it?
    All the darkness swore—acclaim it!

Though the flesh you crooned as sweet
Is sad matter on the street,
    Here's your loam for love and wonder:
    High perfume's a root far under.

In your nights of lightning bloom
Exhalations from the tomb.
    Odds say: stock of man's no bubble.
    So lay faith. But love lay double.

Double? One and one's our three:
I to you, love, you to me
    Were the two wings of one dove
    Radiant moon's the halo of.

Dearest, sleep. Bright night is gone.
Sleep away the dark of dawn.
    Stretch and yawn: your stir and murmur
    Root the entwining ivy firmer.

Plaza de Toros

Madrid. A las cinco . . .

As—for how else do poems go?—as some
Torero in his bravery, gold and red,
Ignites with a playing wrist that ton of plumb
Thunder, all testy rump, hot hovering head—

Toes so, set like a wager, risk a thigh
Bright in its cocky silk, with nerve and bone;
Lids lowered see the terrible horn go by,
And still he rolls like a flag in battle, blown
Crisscrossing—

          Turns a languorous shoulder then
Full on that savage bafflement, in throes.
A rapture of handkerchiefs. Tiptoe, girls and men
Wave till the crowd's in flower, a snowy rose.
Blood on the dust, dark blood on wrist and knee.
"As, you began—?"

          And glory on: as *he.*

The Year, 1520

. . . in the country, not far from Calais . . .

As one who—and so we're a-sonneting?—one who
Sleeps with a casual beauty in the brush:
At morning yawns, amused and tender, "You?
Who are you, stranger?" And the kisses rush.
His finger, reverent, broods on brow, on nose
Tipped with its dust of gold, on flutter of lash.
He jokes at her comb, "A princess?" smoothing clothes
Richer than sundown showed—

                        on a sudden, a flash
Of armor in all the fields around, a thunder
Of oriflammes smarting of smoke and towns afire;
Men-at-arms with hot coals for eyes; and under
Banners, her throne; her ape, her fool and friar.
Hoarse helmets buzzing obeisance raise the girl,
Who sweeps from her cheek, eye blazing, earth and a curl—

Sonnet Almost Petrarchan

And there was that row with the German-Burgundian female . . .

—Canto IX

He stared—lean tusk of a man—and dreamed each breast a
Moon-cameo sheer in silk, her maize hair swaying
Over them as she danced, a glamour playing
In the cool eye that swept his own. *His* fiesta!
He, Sigismondo Pandolfo Malatesta!
Who prettied the church! And she care? Out sashaying!

He splintered the door that night, where those were staying,
Stabbed her young man. Hands, hauling, half undressed a
Glow like the stormy moon's.

                    What, writhe and dare
Breathe deeper to flash effrontery?

                           Flushed, he sunk
—Once, twice—his blade in her shining life. Maize hair
Gagging a cry, she stumbled and—

                        like one drunk
He hunkered: each grunt that frothed in her blood, each hiss
Of animal rapture scavenging: *Kiss! Kiss!*

Design: A Further Word

... If design govern ...

Dull gold of oak leaves falling where they might:
A patch of Byzantium in the undergrowth
For the trillium, white arms dancing—

But, like an oath
Half hissed in a quiet chapel,
this
this sight:
One flower had pierced one leaf, torn it not quite
Apart as the poignant arms would lift. A troth
Dismaying to flower and leaf: one doom for both.
You've heard of a crown of thorns, of a Persian rite
Impaling its victim—stark—in heaven's own light?

Place, time, and weather combined so here:

a-sprawl
On its gibbet inches up, the oak leaf, tight
Spikes into flesh, tormented his blonde upright
Tormenter. A whim of the wind? Or rain's soft fall
Adduced—of the earth's own virtue—vice and awl?

With a Blonde in a Bar-Booth

While you decide, a cigarette for poise?
Your breath inspires it, and your breath destroys.

"Meaning by that?"

                    I only said: Your breath,
The same that gives it glory, gives it death.

"Wait, light me, love. And so—?"

                              What all things say:
Only, how very dark's the end of day.

"Cozy though, here."

                    Inhale! The living spark
Glows till your lip's a lotus in the dark;
Floats you, a rose-gold lotus. Cheeks indrawn.

Well, we're a catch of breath, love. Caught and gone.

A Ballad of Kisses and Combs

When you were a little child, my love,
Silk hair long as you,
Mother gave you a comb and a kiss,
Drew you close as she combed "like this"—
But you ripened out of her arms to his,
Tighter arms than true.

Made a stranger welcome, love,
But he was ill-come there.
You had a kitten teased the fire,
Flowering-snow and a rose in briar—
Played them all on a shy desire,
And the rant of his night-long hair.

Walk away unlucky, love;
Possess the wind and rain.
You had a home, an oaken home,
But his who came was rove and roam—
Much he'd care for the broken comb
Where the bed-length tresses lay.

Walk along the water, love,
Where the salt sea hurls its wave;
Where the woods weave rose in the gold to die,
And dawn from her tumbled dress steps high—
Meadow, easy knee to the sky,
And the blind, deep-kissing grave.

How to Tell the Girls from the Flowers

Both sway. Are fragrant mostly. Wells for dew.
Have their one season early. Tell the two
First by their gaze, half hid with lash or leaf:
Eyes of the girl go deeper. Wells for grief.

A Scholar Wonders

Their human love—confusing! Off they fling
Flurry of skirt, shirt—heavens, everything!
And then, heaped dense and shining, mostly prize
The long long gazing in each other's eyes.

Stewardess Falls from Plane

Unusual bird, unusual words for you?
Earth whistled, and you came. As all girls do.

Daughter, Age 4

Came traipsing to my bed today:
    No other gave so much
Rough-and-tumble tenderness,
    Was such a flower to touch.

Girl of the morning, rowdy rose,
    My own as none was mine
Of those serene and witty ones,
    The tall languorous line,

What's to wish you? (Who's the girl
    Heard any such word said?)
May you, the shapely years at hand,
    Vex such another bed.

Sally and Alison: Julie. And Joan.

Each
so alive with
wind at skirt or curl,
turned, a nice rhyming,
every last girl,
girl of every season
in the changing park,
each? On a date with
marble and the dark?

Vague and
blue April—
love a touchy thing!
Summer: rough sunflowers
scuffle where they cling.
Autumn: fern lash on
cheek a
wild-honey glow—

January, what of her?
Dim, in the dim snow.

April,
if you kiss, no
bird in bush or hand.
August, salt lips that
scour like sea-sand.
Autumn: grain swaying in
arms that gather
rich
and slow—

January, what of her?
  Blind, in the blind snow.

 Take to bed
 April,
and clown away despair.
Summer: such surfing in
 play of seaweed hair!
  Autumn: at dawn all
  offered, soul aglow,
 eyes' amber dance, fern
curling, head to toe—

  January? That girl—?
  In the lost snow.

 April lovers,
 hush them
with a lark in view.
August, by a raw cove
 where the coots halloo.
  Autumn of the
  slow gold
 where the hazel shucks are thick,
poppy lips parted
by a bristled
 rick—

 Crisp: the world turning
whets an edgy air.

Breath of frost? Soon . . .
　somewhere
　　off
　　　there.

　　These knees,
　October,
these to blanch and go—
she,
　our warm breather,
　　wade the waste snow?
　　Not a shrub? Nowhere,
　love, to lie
　　low?

　　Girl
　of every season
in the changing park,
each
　on a date with
　　marble and the dark?
　　Each
　so alive with
wind at skirt or curl,
turned, a nice rhyming,
　every
　　last
　　　　girl
　　　　　?

The Madness in Vermont This Fall

Stripped of its summer wealth,
Can the bough be wan as a root?
Go dingy in spells of frost,
Untrimmed of its bird, its fruit?

No—trees go wild at the thought.
They know what they mean to do.
Wild trees, gone out of your head?
Do you burn to go south, you too?

Are you trying to be fruit, is it that?
Banana, wild cherry, or plum,
Lemon or apricot, grape
Glow of burgundy's from?

Worse, are you envying birds?
Playing oriole, tanager—such?
Long to be tropical wings?
Wildfire in the trees, too much!

Can we keep our heads in a world
With its yankee wit so lost
That the woods are a cry for fire,
And minding the fire is frost?

Love among the Philosophers

And so whan they were a-bedde both, Sir Trystram rememberde hym
of his fyrst love, La Belle Isoude, and suddeynly he was all dismayde,
and other chere made he none but with clyppinge and kyssinge. As for
other fleyshely lustys, Sir Trystram had never ado with her: such
mencion makyth the ffreynshe booke.

You, moody miss who wanted more, recall
Stair stumbled, key sought, fluster in the hall,
Kisses on kisses glistering, and that's all?

Half-heart or whole, we've heart for kissing. True.
Who needs a ffreynshe booke parleying of ado?
It's kissing done, knights-errant pull askew.

When the impetuous soul elects to stray,
The flesh turn sudden saint, and have its day?
Interpret fundamentally *feet* of clay?

Let's speculate—that's our verb now. Fix a drink,
Your hair a mournful oriflamme at the sink.
If links of reason give, why gin's a link.

The soul has claques palavering it's no beast
—Yet roll on the floor so often, at love's feast?
Well, there's the flesh to keep it straight, at least

This virtuous night. No purlieus here to skulk,
Fidelity stalwart in its stubby hulk.
(Not charmed by my *sic* and *ergo,* dear? Must sulk?)

Anatomize *kiss.* Since kissing Judas came
And kissed that kiss of his, they ring the same?
Cold couples kiss and kiss, in Judas' name.

Whereas: that other fleyshely lust, so called,
Longs for a firm affection. Sinks appalled
Seeing itself a stand-in. Though blackballed,

Glum lovely, count your blessings. Science gives
Ghostly advice on chumming with negatives.
(The very stuff we're of, it's water in sieves.)

And: here's a thought rings jubilant in the gloom:
Souls on their own, what noble capers bloom
Seeing old fussy bluenose in the tomb.

As for that vaunted heaven harridans bless,
Crusaders storm, nuns skimp for, who'd take less
Than even dreams of the common couch confess?

Such meditations dazzle: bliss too bright.
Dear, what a shapely yawn. Going early? Right.
Only let's kiss, who never dreamed good night.

Spleen

Catullus, LXX

Well, Catullus. So you knew.
Raged: *what these women coo*

to their lovers, write in air;
find a sea, and write there.

Once I had a girl burned
in my ear words she learned

maybe in a book, or heard
on the loose street slurred.

Tried to write it—one stroke
saw the page curl in smoke.

Wrote it on the air instead:
singing birds fell down dead.

Wrote it on the running wave:
saw the sea fishes' grave.

Roman, here's a better way:
words the pretty lips say,

cut them in your white thigh
for a thought to have by;

gouge a scar fingers find
when the long nights grind;

where, though sweaty limbs thresh,
grief and shame are proud flesh.

A Summer Love

Flourish, with black-raspberry cone

All of us lovers! when the summer sun
pales to the south, and tidy fall's begun,
troop to our rakes and bonfires—off we go,
leaving the gull his bitter kingdom. So:

a keepsake on departure? Of what kind?
What can we give, what something none could find
—no doting husband or fond fussing wife
uncover in some bureau? Found, a knife
(sure as that shoddy rhyme) to either's heart,
the trusting man or woman's. So we part,
no gift but this: bare fistful, purplish, pearled.
Our melting present in a melting world.
Friend of the cool and shady, shy of sun;
kissed away quick by tonguing, quick to run.
Flushed without fervor; without firmness, blunt.
Not to be held—so slipslop—to account.
A thing not meant to last. Nor get us far.

Call it a sort of rhyme for what we are.

Watching the Planes Come in at La Guardia

Joan's kiss
      —it pancakes—
            a flat smack.

                       But Jeanne!
The delicate approach, slow tilt and lean.
All hovering danger and delight.
               As when
Home, over mountain, sea, and chancy weather,
Plane and its shadow
        thrill
           and touch together.

First Date (2)

Be careful whom you kiss. You never know.
Men wade Niagara, upstream, the white flow
Shearing from ankle, shinbone
           —but
             slow . . . slow . . .

The Origin of Myth

For Daphne, decorating the tree

Christmas again. And the kings. And the camels that
    Travel like shanties collapsing. We hurl
        Fistfuls of shivery bliss in the night on a
            Tree like a poised ballerina, that girl

—Well, or one like her—in Ovid: Apollo
    Flushing in shrubs a bent shoulder and head,
        Snorted and plunged for her, lofty blood thundering—
            "Oh," she said. *"Oh!"* she said. There's a girl sped.

Hovered high hurdles; flashed a fine knee or so,
    Flashed a fine—Ovid says, how her flounce flew.
        Cornered, she crinkled to armfuls of laurel, her
            Heartbeat in bark ebbing. Likely: I knew

Much the same story: once scuffled fall foliage;
    Caught the soft runaway, crushed to my brow
        Curls that turned holly leaves, pin-pointy, hissing things;
            Felt the warm bark alive. Heaven knows how

These had gone walking all the broad autumn,
    Poked in gold cubbyholes down the dark run;
        Fumbled in foliage crisp as old tinsel, and
            Tussled and scuffed too much. Blurting: "Been fun."

Fun?—but it wasn't fun. Blundered half purposely
    Into each other—through wool such delight?
        "I want you all," he choked, "cornflower, corn-tassel!"
            "Oh," she laughed, redder then. *"Oh!"* she wept,
                white.

"Snug rough and tumble here? Fun in a furrow bunk?
    What would you do, gamin? Turn to a tree?"
        "I don't know." Tears flickered. "I don't know." Hems
            flinging.
        Whitely defiant though, "Try. And you'll see."

Down the dense calendar's black and red stubble field
    Gone, the October girl. Plunging, he kept
        Eyes on a—cypress? Dead mistletoe? Myrtle-bush?
        Oak that would crash on him? Willow that wept?

Ashen as sassafras? Judas-tree? Juniper?
    Trekking November, he scuffed the dull days.
        Caught her at Christmas, in cedar gloom wassailing.
        Somber, and swirling dark rum as she sways:

"What's a gone girl to you? Better: forever-things.
    All the fall-forest bit; all the dense kiss.
        'Turn to a tree?'" Taking tinsel and bangles, she
        Pinned, in her ponytail, tree-glitter. "This

Crimson for lips, the fall foliage ranting;
    Gold, for that foliage blurred the wind's bliss;
        Blue, for cool gloom in the cornstubble starlight;
        Silver, for lashes lay salt to the kiss.

Bittersweet, mistletoe gussy my goldilocks."
    Arms like boughs bending, she downed the dark rum.
        "Myth's a fine stuff. But won't wear in the dustiness,
        Fetor and stress where the camel-trains come."

Love Song for Outer Space

> . . . that saying of Swedenborg that the intercourse
> of angels is a conflagration of the whole being . . .
>
> —W. B. Yeats

If all that talk of heaven's true
  (Only the grosser whimsy shed:
Cherubs a-larrupin' the lyre,
  Rumps roly-poly overhead),
If glory of consciousness return
  Like morning on the muddled blood,
If we are we, the same we yet,
  And stand together, as we stood,
And take such fire from each, as once
  Set gables of the town ablaze,
Made sootiest dark a dazzle, where
  Fire in the fire we blundered, dazed—
If so—? Blunt stubble of the flesh
  Enkindled beyond power to bear
Ruined us once—and if the soul's
  So combustible essence flare?

Often we had, come dull of dawn,
  Nothing to blend but tepid breath.
Once short of that, we've still in store
  Thrust of the long-careering death.
And: if the heavy flesh could soar
  Of its own weight a handbreath, dear,
And even so touch heaven, quite
  Sprung of its dusty atmosphere,
And casting after, stage by stage,
  Elate propellants, point afar—

If even so from earth, what span,
  Love, in ascension from a star?

Finisterre

And yet a kiss (like blubber)'d blur and slip,
Without the assuring skull beneath the lip.

So the scrivener quilled. In blurry *bluh*'s, such stuff
As charading the flab of flesh, with play enough
On that *kiss* and *skull* for a high sign: love and death
—Two which, the whole world over, catch our breath.
Perpending the two, he sorts their *is,* and *has,*
With many a resonant sequitur, such as:

No way to enfold the flesh and not feel bone.
No way: kiss flesh (poor thing) and you kiss alone.
There's no one home—not a soul. Tang, gusto, glow
Carouse in the skull: heaven's carousel of snow,
Good sleighing one Christmas Eve, Ghost Lake in Maine,
And what you did, age seven, in the rain
Under the maple's tent—no sensual hour
But had its glory in the bone-built tower.

"Tower! There's your old high-horse way! Folks below
Tell: it's a tackier shanty."

                          Even so,
Celebrate—sleek or tousled, in bow, béret,
Goldenhead, towhead, chestnut, raven, grey—
All the world's flurry in your thatchy hut
(There's nothing but old foodstuff in the gut).

Lay your head closer, love. It's world on world
When lips on, up, in, under lips are curled.
Like riding the primal lava!

                    Some such flare
Rolling us, molten, to far Finisterre.
Before us, zodiacal sagas. On we grope,
To be spun in a spangling Nova—there's our hope!

To be spun, like the North's wild lovelocks, round the pole—
Space and time
                    twirl immersing
                                        soul in soul.

from

ZANY IN DENIM

1990

The Consolations of Etymology, with Fanfare

Zany—from *Giovanni* (John),
    Through Venetian *Zanni*.
Denim—from *de Nîmes*. Right on,
    Sing hey nonny nonny!
Once I thought my name—well, blah.
Zany in denim, though! Ta DAH!

The Book of Life

Some puzzle out with finger cramped and slow,
Stay with it long, look backward as they go.
Some read its meaning with immediate eye;
Startled, amused, they laugh. And wave good-bye.

As Goethe Said

Gesellschaft

Aus einer großen Gesellschaft heraus
Ging einst ein stiller Gelehrter zu Haus.
Man fragte: Wie seid Ihr zufrieden gewesen?
»Wärens Bücher,« sagt' er, »ich würd sie nicht lesen.«

Party

Once, at a party, a taciturn prof
Met hordes of new people, but soon hurried off.
When asked how he liked them, their manners, their looks,
Said, "I wouldn't read them, if they had been books."

Hier liegt ein überschlechter Poet.
Wenn er nur niemals aufersteht!

Beneath this stone, an awful poet.
Let's hope to god he stays below it.

Lunch with Old Flame

A pity: the midnight linen, passion's map,
Shrunk to this pallor of napkins in our lap.

Ragdale Haiku

Easy-flowing brook,
Hushed—till root or rock impede.
Then it learns to sing.

Crutches and Canes

Feisty old men, their battle cry a cough,
Waggle their sticks at earth, to warn it off.

Matthew 5:28

"Whoso lusts . . . in his heart . . ." The saying's dire.
Yet some demur: "He's worthier of hellfire
Who, with God's loveliest latest work in sight,
Stifles the radiant impulse of delight."

Disciples

Just one in twelve a traitor? Blessed day!
Since Judas' time, been downhill all the way.

Good Friday

You love us yet? Then really, what a One!
Now that the hustling, hooting, horror's done,
Popped in our pouch of spit, a hot-cross bun.

Poets and Critics

One hound that trots. A thousand fleas that ride.
Which way? A vote for each. The fleas decide.

Verse Translator

Goethe, Racine, Neruda, Pushkin—next!
Some Choctaw? Aztec epic? Or Czech text?
Lo at his touch, as he invades *tromp tromp*,
Mountain on mountain, groaning, turns to swamp.

Occasions of Grace at a Poetry Reading

Thy loving-kindness, Lord! Who, sin to quell,
And keep our souls for heaven, dost show so well
How tedious and interminable is hell.

from

THE SIX-CORNERED SNOWFLAKE
AND OTHER POEMS

1990

The Six-Cornered Snowflake

Strena, seu De Nive Sexangula . . .

❄

The
snows
curleycue
in slow pendulous
❄ pavane, half lured to heaven yet, until ❄
they too concede to earth, drift and accrue
on rugged roofs like plowlands pitched
at odds, akimbo, a mottled-lavender
jumble of old-gold corrugated tile
lofting its crown of thorny towers
over a Prague still Gothic (1610),
Prague not yet voluted with baroque,
aspiring still: see many-steepled Týn!
church-spire on spire like missiles packed
❄ all zeroed in on heaven. Zigzag streets ❄
crevassing seesaw
gables all
round
Týn
❄

❄

Now
zoom
in on "the
incomparable man"
❄   (said Einstein) Kepler, hazy eyes ablink,   ❄
steel mind dividing all heaven like a pie,
whanging the startled orbits till they
rang! Now, this December noon, he's
trudging in snow to see the emperor
out thru the escutcheoned tower's
stone calendar of warrior-saints,
helms, haloes diamonded with snow,
then on to the half-mile windiness of
bridge hurdling the winter river in sixteen
❄   soaring stone leaps, to couch beneath the   ❄
castled heights of
Hradčany
in the
sky
❄

❊

The

steep

question-

mark crook of road

❊ tires him; halfway he'll lounge a while, ❊

look back on the quirky panoramic roofs of

a two-part city the great river splits:

yonder's the Old Town, Staré Město;

here Malá Strana strays: *ma la la la*

K. croons it, the musical Czech name,

eye straying to snow on his coat—

while Emperor Rudolf, head in clouds,

frets in his fabulous attic of retorts,

zodiacs spyglass crucible rubies clocks

❊ Brueghels Dürer—Arcimboldo: royal phiz ❊

abloom in bulbous

fruit thru

goblin

art

❊

❅

But

today

the Royal

Astronomer's late,

❅ hunched there, his mind aswirl with more ❅

than whimwhams of an emperor—all bemused

by signatures of something from above:

the dædal snowflake crystaling in six.

Old thunders roll: "Hast entered

into the treasures of the snow?"

Not yet; but mind is given to know;

the great world to be known. Why six?

Perhaps no reason but exuberant joy?

Pattern's a pleasure; often nature plays

❅ not for rude truth but loveliness of line: ❅

item: this Gothic

mandala's

set of

six

❅

❄
Out
of the
blue, his
thoughts like snow
❄　　flocking in flurries: the black savagery　　❄
of upper air blanched to this flossiness?
Is snow among the amenities of nature,
falling in figures? With Euripides, he
remembers how Polyxena at the tomb,
snowy throat bared, chin tilted for
the sword that trembled more than
she, was "careful to fall decently,"
still minding her skirt now hieroglyphed
with blood. He dreams: over roofs of Prague
❄　　a pale girl floating amid geometries . . .　❄
Fantastical—he's
our myriad-
minded
man
❄

❄

Not

above

a juggler's

way with words, as:

❄ in swank of scholastic Latin *nix* is *snow;* ❄

but, in his burlier German, *nichts* is *nothing.*

Ergo: this snow, like all the world, is

only a pale chemise on nothingness.

You doubt? He'll quote you Persius:

"O curas hominum, O quantum est in

rebus inane." Hollow hopes of men!

One solace though: "A living death

is life without philosophy." Or life

without its drollery: he'll wink at snow's

❄ raunchy role in folklore. "A snowflake ❄

got me with child,"

naughtier

ladies

say

❄

❄
One
grouch,
cornuted
so, totes the tad
❄ south to dispose of, miming in mock woe, ❄
"Your snowflake baby melted in the sun."
Feet shuffle in the decencies of nature.
Meanwhile K. rakes among six-angled
sorts for a clue. In pomegranate?
honeycomb? Prime diamonds mined in
wash of gravel favor octahedrons,
compacted to six peaks—to six, eureka!
Here's earth and sky attuned, a same
sign from each, extruded from blue flues of
❄ long extinct volcanos; from blue choirs ❄
of heaven, the two
choraling
raptly
six
❄

　　　　　　✳
　　　　　All
　　　　primal
　　　forms are
　　hieroglyph: *forma*
✳　means *soul* for the philosophers, as for　✳
　John Dee, sometime astronomer in Prague,
　who saw once in this mirror of a world
　God as "the *Form* of forms." So Kepler
　dreams. To find why forms from *Form*
　scintillate, hover, hold in harmony
　the universe—his passion's there,
　his "only delight." Blear of eye, he
　unriddled optics, made heaven an aviary
of singing planets, bizarre cage in cage,
✳　coped with his Starry Messenger, Galileo,　✳
　but never rightly
　solved the
　why of
　six
　　　✳

❄

Nor

solved

the riddle

of himself, a soul

❄   "like sweet bells jangled": his mother a   ❄

mumbling witch, father a traipsing bravo;

wife in the dumps, babes wailing; great

Tycho dabbing his patchy nose of gold;

feast or famine from the emperor;

a body of scabs and rashes—boils

raw in the saddle, so must trudge

afoot after surly printers set to sue;

then arson, looting, thirty years of war;

his grave obliterated—*this* man attuned

❄   the universe itself in *Harmonice Mundi*?   ❄

made of his quaint

delusions

music

too

❄

❄

We

dream

in neurons.

Form lost in forms,

❄   a blizzard of data blinds our monitors.   ❄

Today, more knowing, we know less. But know

less more minutely. A schoolboy could

dazzle poor Kepler with his chemistry,

chat of molecular bonds, how H:Ö:H

freezes to crystal, the six struts

magnetized by six hydrogen nuclei

(so goes a modern Magnificat to snow)

its six electrical terminals alluring

a bevy of sprightly molecules from out of

❄   weather's nudge and buffeting, the tips   ❄

culling identical

windfalls

of fey

air

❄

❄

Six:

every

petal in

symmetry. And yet

❄   no flake like any other, each enjoying   ❄

a different taste of heaven's variation:

warm, windy, wet, by millimeters, mingle,

freezing molecules till they encode

the millisecond's dharma. Dare we

say, so with us? One muffled moon,

candlelit hands, a half-caught sob,

icon, child's sled, or horseshoe nail

can reassign the history of our days.

"From what Paradisal imagineless metal too

❄   costly for cost" are snowflakes wrought?   ❄

one poet lyricked,

not quite

in K.'s

way

❄

❄
He's
had no
truck with
such "imagineless"
❄ commodities; he loves hang, heft, and edge, ❄
the five Platonic solids scaffolding the
universe. All hollow, yes, but hollow
like calyxes for the essential Dream
that seminates eternity, whose faint
bouquet is the "astounding beauty"
Harmonice Mundi raptures over still,
now, in our late December. Over Prague
of the hundred towers, jumbled roofs,
the winter river, the reconciling bridge,
❄ down our endangered air, forgiving snow ❄
cajoles the earth
in musical
notes
yet
❄

Gravity

Mildest of all the powers of earth: no lightnings
For her—maniacal in the clouds. No need for
Signs with their skull and crossbones, chain-link gates:
Danger! Keep Out! High Gravity! she's friendlier.
Won't nurse—unlike the magnetic powers—repugnance;
Would reconcile, draw close: her passion's love.

No terrors lurking in her depths, like those
Bound in that buzzing strongbox of the atom,
Terrors that, loosened, turn the hills vesuvian,
Trace in cremation where the cities were.

No, she's our quiet mother, sensible.
But therefore down-to-earth, not suffering
Fools who play fast and loose among the mountains,
Who fly in her face, or, drunken, clown on cornices.

She taught our ways of walking. Her affection
Adjusted the morning grass, the sands of summer
Until our soles fit snug in each, walk easy.
Holding her hand, we're safe. Should that hand fail,
The atmosphere we breathe would turn hysterical,
Hiss with tornadoes, spinning us from earth
Into the cold unbreathable desolations.

Yet there—in fields of space—is where she shines,
Ring-mistress of the circus of the stars,
Their prancing carousels, their ferris wheels
Lit brilliant in celebration. Thanks to her
All's gala in the galaxy.

                    Down here she
Walks us just right, not like the jokey moon
Burlesquing our human stride to kangaroo hops;
Not like vast planets, whose unbearable mass
Would crush us in a bear hug to their surface

And into the surface, flattened. No: deals fairly.
Makes happy each with each: the willow bend
Just so, the acrobat land true, the keystone
Nestle in place for bridge and for cathedral.
Lets us pick up—or mostly—what we need:
Rake, bucket, stone to build with, logs for warmth,
The fallen fruit, the fallen child . . . ourselves.

Instructs us too in honesty: our jointed
Limbs move awry and crisscross, gawky, thwart;
She's all directness and makes that a grace,
All downright passion for the core of things,
For rectitude, the very ground of being:
Those eyes are leveled where the heart is set.

See, on the tennis court this August day:
How, beyond human error, she's the one
Whose will the bright balls cherish and obey
—As if in love. She's tireless in her courtesies
To even the klutz (knees, elbows all a-tangle),
Allowing his poky serve Euclidean whimsies,
The looniest lob its joy: serene parabolas.

The Shape of Leaves

A premonition in the leaves,
    old words the forest spoke:
For poplar leaf, read *shield of kings,*
    read *testy rogue* for oak.
Catalpa leaf's a perfect heart;
    your linden leaf, baroque.

Here linden and catalpa drape
    arcades where the entwined
Young hopefuls, dazzled with themselves,
    see all through haloes. Blind,
Good souls, they cannot read the leaves
    or puzzle to construe
Why linden leaf's a crooked heart
    and why catalpa's true,
Or why in fall both turn alike
    to show of goldsmith's art,
Compounding treason in the woods
    —the true, the crooked heart—
Then fallen, mould the earth we know,
    root, humus, tufty growth.

Look, lover: on our weathered jeans
    how rich a stain of both.

Trick or Treat

Holy and hokey, Hallowe'en.
That kindergarten of witches in the street,
Skeletons (but with tummies) doorbell high
Piping up, "Trick or treat!"

A hoyden by Goya with her Breughel chum
Scrabbles black-orange jelly beans—then scoots.
—To think I saw *you,* spangled so,
Rouged, in your Puss-in-Boots

Some forty and more years ago!
Memory: the reruns in full color seem
As three-dimensional as *now.*
Could it be *now*'s the dream

We've been bewitched by?—spirited
Into this crinkled skin, this ashy hair,
Starch at the joints—this hand-me-down
Raggedy gear we wear?

We've dealt with clothes before; know well
Just what they hallow, and how they fall away
Strewing the floor in moonlight; yes,
Into and past midday.

Good costumes then. But now let's play
Pretend with those glittering infants at the door,
Now, that our autumn's come and soon
The snows arrive—before

We're out of costumes and a place to play,
Of zest for the zany carnival in the street,
Out of breath, out of world and time
Teasing with "Trick or treat!"

From the Rapido: La Spezia–Genova

Glossies of Eden? The slim beaches curled
Between rocks and the frill of foam—that's when
There's thunder of tunnels and the underworld.

Pitch-black, down Pluto's flue—till out we're hurled
Back to sea-dazzle and tile roofs' cayenne,
To glossies of Eden, to slim beaches curled

Like sinuous Eve, her lassitudes. The muraled
Villas uphill—it's Steinberg heaven!—then
That shudder of tunnels and the underworld.

But swimtogs merry in blue coves! Their swirled
Piquant revealings—glory be! Amen
To glossies of Eden! to slim beaches curled,

Pavilion, pier, a blazon of towels unfurled,
Twined lovers, barmen, kids, a pup—again
A thunder of tunnels and the underworld.

Books talk of Bede's warm hall, how winter whirled
Through wassailing scops—back into night—that wren,
Sparrow, whatever. But these beaches! curled
So close to abutments of the underworld?

Water Music

῎Αϱιστον μὲν ὕδωϱ . . .

"Nothing noble as water, no,
    and there's gold with its glamor . . ."
Pindar on trumpet—First
    feisty Olympian Ode to the horseman,
Daring us, across the years:
Look to excellence only.
Water, you're pure wonder! here's
February, and on the pane your
    frost in grisaille show how you flowered
    all last summer; it
Stencils clover, witchgrass, mullein
    meadow; between boskage gleam
Shores of Lake Michigan, her snow pagoda, junks of ice.
Farther off, spray and breaker, and your clouds
That hush color to a shadow as they pass,
While snowflakes—just a few—go moseying

Around . . . over . . . That cloud-coulisse
    valentine of a window!
Back of its ferny scrim
    scene after scene of a gala performance!
"Water's Metamorphosis,"
That's the show, and in lights too,
Booking all the world for stage.
Now let's make believe there's a magic
    camera, sensitive only to
    water molecules,
Loading film that blueprints hidden
    wetness in things—profile bold
But pearly the pulp of it: highrise, traffic, elm, marquee
Like electronic pointilliste machines;
On sidewalks, prismatic people, prismy dogs;
Ice-palaces for home. They effervesce

        Of course. Water's alive with light.
            Spawned of the ocean, life's macromolecules

216

Begot history and time;
    culture their afterthought. Our own
Body: mainly bog. Like
    trees walking? No. Walking waves
Are what *we* are. Flesh briny. Our bone-shack sways
    to, smells of, the sea-wrack.
If we're stormy, halcyon too,
    no surprise, with such
Surf, doldrum, and seiche in us.
    Alcoholic? Some.
Water-freaks? Every last one. (All but death,
Old bonehead who, teetotaling, totals all.)
    Thanks to wet ways, we live here.

You've seen films of the Hindenburg?
    Sky afire and the human
Rain from the clouds? But that's
    hydrogen's way: a psychotic companion
Turning—in a flash—berserk.
As for oxygen: sulphur's
Cousin, arsonist, a false
Friend to metal, apt to explode our
    sleepy haze of sawdust or wheat.
    Sickrooms venture its
Name in whispers. Breathe it straight a
    while, and your throat burns, your head's
Logy, disoriented—you're a weakfish gulping sky.
(Nitrogen-thinned, it's breathable.) We've two
Irate djinns here—and what kabbalahs compel
Their spirits to that peace in H_2O?

Strange, that water's a blend of fire
    when it's flame that she hates and
Hisses, her molecules
    angled like arrowheads tooled for a crossbow,
Blunt, just 104 degrees.

Agincourts in the faucet?
Why not? Hi-tech myths can ape
Many an apeman superstition.
    Yet if not twined lovingly—these
    two explosives—my
Wineglass here could turn *grenade*. As
    water reminds us, the world's
A maelstrom of lava beneath her easy circumstance.
All matter's smouldering at the core. Old-
Time Jehovahs—brimstone and the flood on tap—
Might better have let hydrogen relax

        Its double bond to oxygen—
           which would have shown the folk, given folk to show,
        Just who *was* Who, as most
           things evanesced to zero space
        —most, including people.
           Water's our friend. Faucet-flow
        Around finger endears, the way kittens do.
           It blandishes bourbon
        As it mellows (fluid and cube)
           fire to amber, with
        Glass melodies. Diamond, ice
           crystallize alike
        (To the eye); ice though is good-humored, and
        Come spring, will restore playhouse and beach to us,
           melt to mellifluous tilth.

Besides, diamond's a liar—*poof*
    and it's soot when the heat's on.
Calling their glaciers back,
    Ice Ages warmed to us, left the lea greener.
What would Diamond Ages do?
Shrink-wrap countries in rock-glass,
Leave the planet strangled, sky's

Lavaliere, a Tiffany bijou
   glinting frigid fire. And would you,
   Diamond-Age young girls,
Cherish dewdrops, think them jewels to
   pretty your hair with—eyes brave
Through the damp of your lash before the livid avalanche?
Let's be glad—most of us anyway—we're
More dew-sort than diamond-kind. And there's the myth:
What suckled Aphrodite, sea or stone?

Festooned Sicily shore?—where foam,
   all glissando and swell, wreathes
Buoyant the swimmer. Dream:
   eastward in Eden once sparkled a garden
More delicious even than
Sappho's: apples blew perfume
Through liana languors; brooks
Wove their watery spell; mid-grove a
   Presence walked in cool of the day.
   No one dewier
Than that human pair, pellucid
   two, in the sun-flickered shade
By the pools, on a ferny tussock banked like pouffes. No one
Dewier? *You* were! that rickety pier
Once! your shoulders bubbling moonlight as you swam
And then—spirit of water, lithe—gleamed bare

     As moon on the pier, hair swirled back,
       laughing at me, "Last one in . . . !" Prismatic girl
     (Like those glorified trans-
       lunar dancers that Dante saw)
     Sprinkling me with chill lake's
       mischievous fire. Now the tears
     Are like fire to think . . . think . . . what I've thought and thought.
       But safer to think small:

Summer thunder, hail on the lawn;
    cuddling scotch-and-hail,
We blessed it as "heaven-sent!"
    Mostly water is.
Pray that it keep us. Our blue globe in space.
Our grand loves. Our least ones—like this spindly rose
    rambling on Pindar's lattice.

Dropping the Names

Alps, island, jet, crest, logo—Barnum's own
Chromos on luggage of the lives we led.
Contessa, in the Mercedes toward Chinchón,
Remember, the day of the bullfight, what you said?—
When, ruffling back your curls' mahogany gloss
(The cub reviewer enthused, "Pompeian torrents!")
You showed me a cheek glass hail had marked, crisscross,
The night your Ferrari was crumpled north of Florence;
And, mocking yourself, emoted, "My 'career'!
My dreams of *Vissi d'arte!* Doomed? In ashes?"
As—I don't think before or since—one tear
Glistened, a moment's diamond, in your lashes,
Gleamed and was gone. Then lightly, "'*Cosa fatta.* . . .'
—Remember Dante? It's true our blossoms blow
Away too early? Except forget-me-not. Ah,
Non ti scordar di me!"
                               The words we know!
The words we know, to cherish and forgive in,
Console us when their referents go wrong.
Afford, somehow, a sort of world to live in
(So leaden hours are alchemized in song).
Not words to post on luggage. Hardly posh there.
Your palm cajoled my right hand from the wheel,
Lay in it, easy.
                         Later, in the crush there,
We parked, sipped our *anís*—then bugles peal.
Curls—their autumnal luster!—veiled a cheek
Your finger questioned still; eyes twilight-blue
Mused on the crowd, the rough-and-tough, the chic
—Gina was there and, word went, Ava due
Down from Madrid. No bullring, so they made
A planked-in plaza of the village square,
Ramshackle stands that lurched as we *¡Olé!*d;
Gazers from rooftop, window, everywhere
And often eyes on you, who'd known that town
From childhood, stranger from your Umbrian hill

At first, then friend to many up and down
Those streets, most every fall. And special still.

Nothing went wrong, that day, at the wild rites.
Nothing—that day. We've seen the manshape flung
Dark on the sky for all his suit of lights,
Or from the horn, an endless second, hung.
And we've seen more: death's rubric on the sand
Beneath the sky's wide innocence of blue.
But nothing that day. Still, I kept your hand,
Saw the half sucked-in smile, and knew you knew
Moments of truth too blinding to expect
Unless one wore the initial on her cheek,
His mark, the new possessor, who'd collect
His own in time. His time. We didn't speak
Much in that numbing razzmatazz, that spree of
Dicey heroics. But my sidelong gaze
Felt a remoteness in your soul—as free of
Burdens, concerns bedeviling our days.
Remoteness? Hardly! Not by *sol* or *sombra*.
—Lightness, a buoyancy of hawsers cut
Is what I felt. More aureole than penumbra,
Much as you were, through all the days we—

                                            but
You nudged me, "Nearly over. Let's be going.
Away from crowds." Once through them, with head high,
You led to a *glorieta*—there, boughs blowing,
A flurry of poplar leaves from the loose sky
Hoo'd at us, hustled us, tourbillions pulling
This way and that . . .
                    then, withered,
                              . . . off in wind . . .
Leaves colorful as comics. Luggage peelings
Of island, alp, jet, logo—paper-thin.

The Wine of Astonishment

> Thou hast shewed thy people hard things: thou hast
> made us to drink the wine of astonishment.
>
> —Psalm 60:3

In a cozy booth at noon,
Musky wine our pleasure. Soon,
Touch of finger, touch of knee
Terminals of circuitry
—Long we loll, as in our eyes
Jane and Tarzan socialize.

> One more for the road, and so
> Sleekly overboard we go
> Drifting off amid a kiss
> —Surfers ride a sea like this.

Crowding close (as couplets do
Huddling unheroic too)
Onward we meander, twined.
We're a sight—but never mind.
Look, they circle wide from us,
Homefolk herding for the bus.
Don't they know it's virgin spring?
Know we're put on earth to sing?

> Who says bubbly life goes flat?
> Rites of noon chant, Hell with that!
> Didn't Solomon himself
> Shimmy at the liquor shelf?
> And his tuneful kin take part
> With, "Wine maketh glad the heart?"
> Didn't vivid saints in Spain
> Just to put the matter plain
> Liken love, when most divine,
> To enrapturings of wine?
> (Ours, *de la Grange Abélard,*
> Memories of the mazy Loire.)

Now where are we, you suppose?
Headstones huddle, rows on rows
—It's a marble orchard! Scary?
No, it's grassy, shady, airy.
In their model digs, the dead
Keep their place, with, at their head,
Slabs of data—ups and downs
Mimicking our taller towns.

Raw geometry, these stones:
Knob and bobbin, spire and cones
So unlike what went below—
Bodies with their to-and-fro
Sassy amorous ado,
Curve and curl and—well, like you.

But these chunky stone-folk? No!
Never! Not the way to go.

Though no curfew toll the knell,
City sirens do as well.
Trying out a slab for size
Once the tribal tears are shed,
What's death but a change of bed?
Darling, we've changed beds before,
So who minds the darker door?
Didn't lanes of deeper dark
Counsel lovers where to park?

Tricking out our *death* as *bed*
Doesn't hold for *dying*. (Dread
Veils it—chilling and obscene.)
"Lovely . . . soothing Death" I mean,
What the good grey poet chants,
Slop pail in the frowzy plants.

As for shucking bodies off,
Dowdiness (ask any prof)
Comes of wearing entropy
—Shake away the stuff! Get free!

Garments flung aside before
Lay at bedtime on the floor,
Lay there as the naked went,
Breathless, to love's stark event.
Things that happened many a night
Led us to the heart of light.
Though I won't say, quite, the Cloud
Of Unknowing. Not aloud.

In your gloriole of curls
Once you woke, the way of girls,
—Breasts, in candor of a yawn,
Like originals of dawn—
Stretching, kicked the sheets away,
Sat up laughing, "Why it's *day!*"

That's the way it's going to be.
Proof? I've proof galore in me.

Further proof before we close?
Einstein, Planck, de Broglie, those
Ardent spirits, tuned so fine
On the headiest of wine,
Once, in ecstasies of mirth,
Flicked the seven veils from earth.
Unappareled, as in dream,
They saw meadow, grove, and stream,
Saw our every pleasure spot
The reverse of what it's not.

Shucking duds of circumstance,
Nature did her naked dance.

Einstein, in a fit of glee,
Found a gaudy teaser: E
$= mc^2$. That m
Means our *mass* of flesh and phlegm.
m's why, trying as we might,
We can't touch the speed of light.
m's for *mortal* too—old troll
That's a drag on time and soul.
Flesh succumbing, off it drops
And we're spry as light! Time stops.

     In effulgence of pure c,
     There remains—? Elysian *E!*
     Energy at speed of light—
     What a way to spend the Night!

          Madcap saint, Teresa, she'd
          Tell of *terrifying speed,*
          Of *velocidad . . . temor*
          In the spirit set to soar;
          There's no *bullet from a gun*
          Sped like soul at take-off—none.
          Bullet? Gun? Castilian truth
          Wants *pelota, arcabuz.*
          Ávila and Amherst—nuns
          Making with the loaded guns?

Speed that's incandescence. There,
All the facts of when and where,
Earth and every common sight
Bonded as coherent light,
Broken symmetries of earth
Tuned in unison. It's worth
Claiming we're forever! So
Blow the moment till it glow.

Even sound and sense concur:
Obit's snug in *obiter.*

Spirits—raki, sake, kvass—
Sing, *In vino veritas.*
Tavern wisdom. Old *da·guerre·o·-*
type of motto. But, *In vero*
Est vinositas—there's truth
With the zingo! zest! of youth.

Our way's rocky. To begin it
Take a truth with relish in it.

Dear? You're miffed? Toe tapping while
Lightnings flicker in your smile?

"You're so funny, love! So phony!
Such an upchuck of baloney.
You a *thinker*? That's your angle?
You—with head all jingle-jangle?
We don't need such hocus-pocus.
Noon put everything in focus.
Muscadet's a lovely laser.
Cat's pajamas. Occam's razor.
In the spring, are lips for talking?
Use them right. Then let's get walking."

Well . . . *then!* To our cozy booth
For another round of truth.

Hospital Breakfast: With Grace After

I

Waking in drifts of whiteness: head to toe
I'm a white sheet, with all but nose below.
Toes ripple, push, make corners; the sheet pulls tight
Until I'm hemmed in a box here, with four right
Angles and four straight edges, as if I lay
Chalky—

A skirt swirls. And the breakfast tray!

All's orange: dawn at the window, juice I drink.
"Carols of Florida in that golden ink,"
Croons fever, loony. And egg-yolks bobble, most
Like the sun's globe through cirrus. Tussle of toast
That tugs in the teeth. Blonde slinky marmalade—

Lord, what a world the Lord of matter made!

Breakfast—that daily "He is risen!"—swirls
Its color, tang, aroma—cozy as girls
Leaning bare shoulders over, warm hair loose . . .

In breakfast such epiphany? Joy in juice?

II

We, trivial, live by trifles. Froth: our race
Vague as a drift of atoms, in blind space?
Earth offers "neither joy, nor love, nor light,
Nor certitude . . ."

Was Arnold *real*?

Not quite.

Let's venture—for what's to lose?—a breakfast prayer
To the great Thought that dreamed us—if it's there.

St. Peter once went surfing and he scored
Riding his big feet only—look, no board!
Once, strong souls walked on water; were ultra-tough
Sag-free conniption-proof all-weather stuff.

We're not like those. But, wreathed in gulls and kelp,
Would ruffle the tidal shallows. Peter, help,
Help us to scrabble over wrack and sand
Alongshore toward—

                      some distant lighthouse?—
                                    and

To dangle (though water-walkers all are gone)
Our toes in the froth and glamors of the dawn.

Elegy

For Marion, for Jane

I   Death and the Maiden

Were you, as old prints have shown,
armor over props of bone,
scythe like scorpion tail a-sway,
here's a word or two I'd say:

When you met that lady now
—her of the amused cool brow—
which of you with more an air
carried off the occurrence there?
Held—the buoyant head so high—
every fascinated eye?
Stole, as half in mischief too,
scenes *you* strutted front to do?

Which at last, when curtains met,
had us leaning forward yet
in the dark?—to breathe and rise,
odd elation in our eyes?

II   "One Day Anyone Died I Guess"

Here she lies, poor dancing head,
in the world we know of, dead.
Every sense avers: The End.
Yet we're hedging (who'd pretend
our five portholes on the night
gauged the seven oceans right?)
hedging: past a world in stream,
past the learned journal's dream
(quark or quasar, beta ray),
what's that glimmer? limbs at play?
Something there? a curtain stirred?
Laughter, far and teasing, heard?

Where such awesome laws are set,
Honey, misbehaving yet?

Keeping Change

Handfuls of change,
Squirreled away, half my life, across
The world, in every strange
City I'd mosey in, a week, a year—
Odd coins I'd pocket, toss
Into a box now flop-eared, straggle here
Strewn on the desk, some crisply cut,
Some thumbed and blunt—flag, owl, ship, dolphin—who knows what?

For years ignored
On their high closet shelf, a stash
Of frizzled racquets, hoard
Of postcards, photos, love notes (old-rose stamp
Her tongue-tip curled to!)—cache
I've spread to reckon with beneath the lamp.
They say "Memento!" and I must,
Leaning to puff away the annuities of dust.

Time's stray parade:
Duce, Reich, junta, *coups de main;*
Legend, adventure, trade;
Copernicus, hula-hooped in star and sun;
At moonstruck keys, Chopin;
The wingèd horse, two breeds: the Italian one
Circus-bred, flighty—off he's flown!
Savvy cayuse the Greek—the hind hooves slash at stone.

Auras of ghost
(Gamy, the old folk's rumor ran,
Like bonfire myrrh, almost)
Rose from dead flesh congealing in its bed:
So, in this graven clan,
What's rotten dies; a fragrance lifts instead:
Mere slugs once for the bought-and-sold,
They're soul's own specie now, her special gloss of gold.

Demonetized
(That's *demon* in a cage, and so
Means evil exorcised?),
Their curse is scoured in time's salt vat, the sea's
—The curse that dogged us, "No
Good thing is ever done for such as these.
Where these insinuate, our face
Changes, and smiles go sly—our mettle too is base."

These innocents
Have quit commodity for good,
Shrugged off the purse-and-pence
To ponder—as lips that pore on lore of lips—
What blessed them while it could,
The fostering palm, disbursing fingertips.
Relics, you conjure far too much:
Ardor our fingers felt, curled palms they burned to touch.

Now Hanukkah
Entwines in fire the Syrian kings;
The romp Veronica
Swirls in a bright bewilderment of bulls.
Hands rummage all such things
For clues: no wonder a djinni in metal pulls
My thought to pole or pole: *when? where?*
We had transaction, once. Our futures, all, cried fair.

The *złoty* here
Means Vistula starlight, bush and bank
In shadow, no one near
But each near, nearer each—that *near*'s a fire
Poor hearts hope nuclear. Thank
This *drachma* then for Delphi: our desire
Raced where the naked runners' sweat
Spattered the sod where once our soft intaglios met.

These *krónur* stand
For thunder in Iceland, what we'd do
In that black-lava land
Volcanoes scrunched. We read volcanoes right.
Read them? Well! *were* them too,
Hotel room dancing to our lava light.
That corridor of doors—gone gray?
Pipes from a primal fire heat Reykjavík today,

Won't warm us, though.
Fire's out—that's scarier than *Fire!*
At least the young thought so.
The coins we tossed, fresh-minted, how they spun,
Dates glittering! Dates expire,
And with them all things current in the sun.
Dates love the dust and pile it deep.
Friend, keep your "Keep the change"—change being all we keep.

Palinode

So, the well-known gamut run,
    Love, hate, rage, despair,
He awoke one morning, free,
    Breathed a cleaner air.
Bolt upright in bed he laughed:
    Not a phantom there.

Sat and laughed, and whole of heart
    Damned the pale girl then,
She whose beauty broke that heart;
    Damned the careful men.
Hugged his fate that gave a heart
    Time could break again.

Hearts that finish life entire,
    Hearts the rank and sweet
Never cramped in agony,
    Rode roughshod that beat—
What's that thing? A human heart?
    Throw the dogs that meat!

Throw it to the pale girl then,
    Let her pink and blue
Beauty mumble at that rag
    When the dogs are through—

       Cossack, waste that brutal tongue!
        Or go gargle glue!

       Knowing: there were touches once
        —Likely not again—
       Knowing: many a time she left
        All the world of men,
       Curled so close—oh none could tell
        Sobs from kisses then.

What's for comfort? Stout cliché
    That locks lovers tight:
Earth's a whirligig; blue noon
    Riddled with black light;
See the very sun, our saint,
    Waltz with lurid night.

Niagara

I

Driving westward near Niagara, that transfiguring of the waters,
I was torn—as moon from orbit by a warping of gravitation—
From coercion of the freeway to the cataract's prodigality,
Had to stand there, breathe its rapture, inebriety of the precipice . . .

Fingers clamped to iron railings in a tremor of earth's vibration,
I look upstream: foam and boulders wail with a biblical desolation,
Tree roots, broken oar, a pier end, wrack of the continent dissolving . . .

Braced, like tunnel workers hunching from implosion of locomotives,
I look down: to ancient chaos, scrawl of the fog for commentary,
Misty scripture—Delphic, Jungian—all mythology in gestation,
Mists that chill our face in passing, soar to a mushroom luminescence . . .

In between, where halos dazzle—as, on a high wire, spangled dancers—
On the brink those waters sluice to, in the devil-may-care insouciance
Of their roistering to glory, no forewarning of what impends, till
Solid earth dissolves beneath them; all they had banked on once, vacuity . . .

Kindled in the hollow wind they flare to a greenish incandescence;
Channels they defined so smartly in the gusto of their careering
All behind them now; before them, blinding haze and the noon's diffusion . . .

II

Ten feet over those, our railing perched on a spur where verge and void—there!—
Hiss and arc to touch each other, matter and shadow-matter fuming,
We stare through the flow to bedrock, flashing its Kodachrome geology.
Images swirl by—real, fancied—bits of hallucinated litter:
Gold of oak leaf, taffy wrapper, lavender airmail—assignation?
Yellow Kodak pack, pied comics, tissue a crimson lip had stippled
(Let's imagine). Some shows vivid, fresh-shellacked in the river's sepia,
All no sooner seen than vanished—on to the brink, its foaming rotors
Hoarse as all earth's turbines turning in a thunder of synchronicity.
How deep toward the edge? waist? shoulder? as through a woozy lens we scan its

Floor, old temple tesselation—

                    No, terrain of the moon! Medusa's
Ancient face, and we stare frozen: stony glare in its vipers' tangle . . .

Still a thought returns and troubles: "no forewarning of what impends, till—"
Shadow of *impends*—more menace coiled in the word than fact itself has:
Fact erodes in action: Athens, in the arroyos of her theater,
Leaned to watch the self-destructing of her blinded grandiosities,
Willfulness and Will, a crash course; then, too late for it, anagnorisis;
Purged of trivia through immersion in the clotted baths of tragedy,
Then she knew and was transfigured by contrarious exaltations . . .

III

Eyes can't leave the livid seething, its reiterative *Memento!*
Reading, in this bubble chamber, stuff of the world as effervescence,
Reading every life as half-life, reading in foam the one prognosis . . .

Mac the trucker—checkered mackinaw, sort of a baseball cap with earflaps,
Fists to crinkle up his beer cans—here at the falls is philosophical:
"Down the tube. That's life"—he's waggish, nudging his cozy blonde—"You
                                               know, hon?"
And she knows. We all know: Nature, making a splendor of our banalities,
Lavishes Niagara on us, nudging our knack for the anagogical . . .

Meanwhile, earth itself rolls over, nations caught in its tug of traction,
From the brink of noon to darkness (but the grandeur of the transition!)
Gone, like taffy wrapper, tissue:
                              ferny world of the stegosaurus,
Heraclitus, toe in rivers, Coriolanus in Corioli,
Dancing T'ang girl, belles of Bali, kings of France with the Roman numerals,
Gone, the fripperies and follies glossed in an *Architectural Digest,*
Halls of mortuary marble, dinky glitz of the rare *objet,* the
Aubusson, netsuke, scrimshaw, Tiffany, Tanagra, Bokhara,
All things *au courant,* things current—what a word with the gorge before us!—
All our bookshelves, facts in folio, paleontology, agronomy,

Jewels from that cluttered dump, statistics—

                                many a scuffed Aladdin's lamp there:
As: one cell's genetic lore'd fill seventy-five Manhattan phone books;
As: for each poor soul among us, many a galaxy out there somewhere,
Each of us more precious—rarer!—than a glittering island universe . . .

We could catalogue forever; there's no end to the world's diversity,
All that affluence from somewhere, more than a continent behind it;
There's no diminution either from the torrential cornucopia
Since that primal burst of fireworks, first explosion from singularity;
All the *things,* their scree, diluvium—go to the malls for confirmation:
Lurid brass shop, teak shop, tech shop, patio 'n' pool shop, campy duds shop . . .

IV

Most we're through with soon enough, but some! how they lacerate the heart—not
Savage indignation's gash—but thrilling, with finer blade, pain's inmost
Nerve: the unsigned card *I love you* kept in a bureau drawer for decades;
Sweater she wore once, that autumn, rich with the campfire musk; then letters,
Lavish *o,* impulsive flourish, "When you're away, in other cities,
It's their weather reports I look for, first thing in the morning papers . . ."
So once the Provençal poet, in his rapture about *freid' aura:*
"Winter winds that blow from your land

                            feel like heaven upon my cheek here . . ."

They've gone too, Provence and poet, off in the jumble-carts of history,
Who was *she?* that rueful beauty, jewel of the court and joy of kings, who
Dying murmured, "Je me regrette!"—wistful dear, with her curls disheveled
On that last of all her pillows, feeling the dark impend—"I'll miss me!"
Images swirl by: châteaux that dance in the pool's hallucination,
Fêtes and follies effervescing—champagne, glass, and the hand that held them—
Last, herself, the self where soul is, world of her lavalieres and lovers.
Did she dream, through mists arising, how on the high wire, floodlit dancer,
She had lived her brilliant moment? Hear, as the blood ran hushed, sonorous
Thunders of the living river, more than a continent its source? And
Not divine—so near the brink where verve like hers and the void meet, seething—
Wreathed in opulence of sunset, some transfiguring of the waters?

Closed for Restoration

Our gaudy years in Italy! In between
Those years and now, some thirty. I'm back today.
Eye, stride (and finger in guidebook) still as keen
—Only, rebuffed by barriers. *Ma perché?*
Brancacci Chapel? The Borromini dream,
Our shiver of pleasure? San Clemente's floor?
The monster's Golden House, weird walls agleam?
All? *Chiuso per restauro* against the door,

Giving us pause. Odds are, I'll never see
That span again. If on Liguria's shore
I lie, *Qui dorme in pace*'s not for me,
Stones with *le ossa* . . . or *tristi spoglie* . . . or
Any such dismal lingo of the lost.
Mine, *Chiuso per restauro.* With fingers crossed.

NOTES

"The Beautiful Atheist"

The epigraph translates as "A little song in the air."

"Trivia"

The epigraph translates as "In a place where three roads meet."

"Trainwrecked Soldiers"

The Greek in the last stanza translates as "Alas! Alas!"

"Polonaise"

The epigraph translates as "Goodnight, Love . . . / Remember of me a little longer." Stanza 2: Biskupin is an ancient lake settlement in western Poland. One can still see remains of the primitive huts in the marsh.

"Roman Letter"

The epigraph translates as "or who had adorned life by refining the arts and deserved fame for themselves" (*The Aneid*, book 6, lines 663–4).

"A Frieze of Cupids"

The epigraph translates as "Who on the barren spine / of the dreadful mountain / Vesuvius the Destroyer."

"And a Fortune in Olive Oil"

Two or three of the sonnets in this group may occasionally be a little remote in their allusions. "And a Fortune in Olive Oil" will be clear to those who have read a little about ancient science. Thales of Miletus, born about 624 B.C.E., has been called the founder of geometry, which he introduced into Greece from Egypt. "Being twitted with a lack of practical sense, he confounded his critics by making a fortune in olive oil. This he did by renting all the olive presses in an off season, foreseeing a big crop, and then renting them out at high rates"(Benjamin Farrington, *Greek Science,* 1:31). Thales's theory that the world originated in water is said to mark the beginning of physical science. He "sweetened" the world by looking at it in terms of reason rather than of myth and superstition, as in Babylonian and Egyptian thought. Ur and Lagash were, like Babylon, cities in the Fertile Crescent. Line 4 refers to Babylonian myth; lines 5–8 to Egypt. Thales appears in line 9; he looked at the world through "aqueous humor," the medical term for the fluid in the eye (he used his eyes to investigate nature). It also suggests his theory of cosmology. Lines 11–12: Thales measured the height of the pyramid by comparing the relationship between his shadow and his true height to that between the pyramids' shadows and what he estimated was their true height. "Huffed gilas" are the gila monsters of superstition, which exploded into nothingness when Thales made his discoveries.

"Calliope to Clio"

The epigraph is the opening lines of *The Iliad:* "Of the ruinous wrath of Peleus' son Achilles, which brought many griefs to the Achaians, sing goddess."

"Conclusion"

The epigraph translates as "That which is scattered through the universe bound with love in a single mass."

"The Observatory Ode"

This poem (the Harvard Phi Beta Kappa poem, 1978) might be described as concerned with relations between reason and imagination, fact and fable, theory and myth—*science and poetry*. And about how the view of the universe suggested by modern science is a kind of magnificent myth—or poem.

Stanza 2: Percival Lowell (1855–1916), the brother of Amy Lowell, was the Phi Beta Kappa poet at Harvard in 1889. A writer on Japanese and Korean culture, he later devoted himself to astronomy, particularly at the Lowell Observatory at Flagstaff. He thought that the "canals" on Mars were part of an irrigation system that showed the planet was inhabited. Perturbations in the orbit of Uranus (and of Neptune) convinced him that there was a Planet X beyond them. In 1930 a planet was indeed found so close to the place he predicted that he is generally given credit for the discovery. The planet was named Pluto in his honor.

Stanza 3: The Harvard College Observatory began in 1875 to employ women as "computers," to study, classify, and catalogue thousands of stars from photographic plates. By 1919 forty such women had given seven hours a day, six days a week, to this highly skilled and demanding work. "Learns that *how bright* can mean *how far*" refers to Henrietta Swan Leavitt's discovery of the "period-luminosity law": her careful measurement of variable stars in the Small Magellanic Cloud suggested a correlation between true brightness and rate of variation. This was an important clue to the real distance of the star and hence to the real size of the universe.

Stanza 4: Such researches as those of the Harvard women and Lowell (who seems to have worked himself into a state of nervous exhaustion) led to the view of the universe and its origin that many—probably most—scientists hold today. From the explosion of the primal fireball came (eventually) the stars whose core burned at such a temperature that thermonuclear reactions produced the elements we know. Great explosions scattered the elements into space, where (eventually!) they fell together into such galaxies and systems as our own, with the world we live in.

"Slapstick I"

The epigraph translates as "that purpled, puckered mouth." Catullus was apparently the first Roman writer to employ the word *basium,* from which is derived the word for *kiss* in several Romance languages.

"The Year, 1520"

One possibly relevant event of 1520 was the spectacular meeting of Henry VIII and Francis I of France at the Field of Cloth of Gold near Calais. Neither monarch figures in the fable.

"Sonnet Almost Petrarchan"

"That row" in which Pound's hero Malatesta was involved consisted of his murdering a beautiful woman, who had rejected him, and then violating her corpse—or so Malatesta's enemies asserted.

"Design: A Further Word"

Cf. Frost's sonnet "Design."

"Love among the Philosophers"

The epigraph is from Sir Thomas Malory's *Le Morte d' Arthur*.

"The Six-Cornered Snowflake"

In 1610 Johannes Kepler was living not far from Týn Church in Prague's Old Town (Staré Město), the section to the west of the Vltava River. One day, crossing the famous Charles Bridge—begun in 1357 and, with its great bridge-towers at either end, still a tourist attraction—he noticed the snowflakes on his sleeve and again wondered, as men had for centuries, why they were always hexagonal. In views of Prague from the time, we can trace the rest of his walk: passing through the Little Quarter (Malá Strana) at the far end of the bridge, he began his climb up to the heights of Hradčany *(hród-chany)* and the palace of the Emperor Rudolf II, the reclusive and eccentric collector of great art and of curiosities of every sort—among them his master of ceremonies, the painter Arcimboldo, who did the emperor's portrait as an assemblage of fruits, grains, and vegetables. Kepler had come to Prague some years before at the urging of the astronomer Tycho Brahe, who, having lost his nose in a duel, had replaced it with the gold and silver one, which it is said he kept dabbing with an ointment he carried.

Kepler's wonderment about the snowflakes led to his writing a charming little book in Latin, *De Nive Sexangula*, as a *Strena* or New Year's gift for a patron. In it the author, who knew the classics well enough to write poetry in Latin, does quote Euripides. Elsewhere, on more than one occasion, he quotes Persius, one of his favorite poets. Kepler of course had no way of knowing what we know now about snowflakes: the single flakes are hexagonal because of the molecular behavior of freezing water. But he has some witty and original observations about their form and about form in general. The poet who "lyricked" the lines quoted in stanza 11 is Francis Thompson, in "To a Snowflake."

Stanzas whose shape imitates that of the object they describe go back at least to the ancient Greeks, who called the practice *technopaignia*. Often they are little more than what that name means: "technique-play." But sometimes, as in George Herbert's "Easter-Wings," in which the lines expand and contract with the thought, the shape itself can dramatize what is being said. Thoughts about snowflakes and their shape seemed to offer the once-in-a-lifetime chance to make use of what is graphic in typography. Technical specifications: in the hexagonal stanzas, the three equal axes between opposite points intersect in 60-degree angles at their center.

"Water Music"

The epigraph is taken from Pindar's Olympian Ode I and translates as "water is best." Somewhere in the course of my thinking about doing a water poem, what is probably Pindar's most famous line came into my head. I looked up the rhythm of the ode in which it occurs, wondering if his complicated Greek meters could be transposed into our accentual system. English writers (like Goethe and Hölderlin on the continent) had adapted the more familiar Greek meters, but I could not think of anyone who had taken the prosodic pattern of a Pindaric ode as the metrical substructure of a poem in English. It was a challenge: interest in form is more adventurous if one tries to do new things with it. As Pound knew, one way to "make it new" is to resuscitate something so old that everyone has forgotten it.

The "Pindar's lattice" on which this poem is grown is the quantitative-syllabic grid of his "First Olympian Ode," with the long and short Greek syllables transposed to our accented and unaccented ones. Key rhythmical elements are the *glyconic* (× × — ∪∪ — ∪ —) as in line 1, and the *pherecratic* a catalectic form of the *glyconic* (× × — ∪∪ — —), as in line 6. (The ×'s mark syllables that are "common," either long or short.) Other rhythmical elements are related to these. All are forms of *logædic* or "speech-song," combinations of dactyls and trochees felt to be somewhere between prose and verse. The meters of individual lines vary within what we might call the stanzas; corresponding lines in the 16-line strophe and antistrophe have the same meter. The 15-line epode (every third "stanza," indented) has its own pattern. Some sequences that work out in Greek cannot very well be carried over into English: line 13 of strophe and antistrophe, for example, begins with seven short syllables in a row. In English seven unaccented syllables together are unlikely, or probably even impossible, except in some such jokey line as "'B-b-b-b-b-b-but . . .' he stammered." One advantage of using such an accentual-syllabic grid is that it offers the writer the best of two worlds: to a listener (or reader) his poem may sound as free as prose, but to the writer comes the satisfaction of knowing that he is following, syllable by syllable, accent by accent, a form as rigorous as the chemical affinities of nature are.

"Niagara"

The rhythm of this poem was suggested by the galliambic meter of Catullus 63 (a translation of which, in galliambics, may be found in the third edition of my *Sappho to Valéry: Poems in Translation,* University of Arkansas Press, 1990). The Latin poem, though its content has nothing to do with "Niagara," is worth recalling here for its own sake. In it, Catullus gives us his version of the story of Attis, the Phrygian fertility figure that corresponds to the Syrian Adonis. Attis, in a fit of religious mania, castrates himself for the goddess Cybele—and lives to regret it. As Frazer writes in *The Golden Bough,* "When the tumult of emotion had subsided, and the man had come to himself again, the irrevocable sacrifice must often have been followed by passionate sorrow and lifelong regret. This revulsion of natural human feeling after the frenzies of a fanatical religion is powerfully depicted by Catullus in a celebrated poem."

One thing that caught my interest in the poem was its curious rhythm. Gilbert Highet, in *Poets in a Landscape,* says the meter is "fantastically difficult . . . the rhythm of the eunuch's savage dance, on which he plays many subtle variations." L. P. Wilkinson, in *Golden Latin Artistry,* says, "The Galliambic meter was invented to express . . . the orgiastic dance to Cybele—the essentials beneath the variations are the anapaestic tread of the wild dance and the short rattling syllables of the tambourine or castanets at the end." The meter is basically:

$$\cup\cup - \cup \mid - \cup - - \mid \cup\cup - \cup\cup \mid \cup\cup\underline{\cup}$$

Catullus takes the usual metrical liberties: two shorts for a long; a long for two shorts, reversed syllables, etc.

For years, probably for two or three decades, I had been teased and haunted by this rhythm, wondering if, with its quantitative basis changed to our qualitative one, it could be made to serve any purpose in English. The only poem I knew that did try it in our language was Tennyson's "Boädicea," which the poet said was a "far-off echo" of the galliambics of Catullus. Because of the meter, he published it among "Experiments." With lines that speed up at the end, it does have the feeling of the galliambic movement, but Tennyson does not try consistently to follow its pattern. William Harmon later called my attention to George Meredith's "Phaethon," which Meredith said was "Attempted in the Galliambic Measure."

I am not sure how "Niagara" first fell into this rhythm. I may have been attracted by the sweep and amplitude of the long line. At some point I came to think the meter appropriate for my subject, since in a way the poem is concerned with, among other things, solidity and dissolution. After the solid first half of the line, the second half seems to rush away in a flurry of quick syllables. These had forced Catullus into using or even making up words not found elsewhere in Latin: *bederigerae, properipedem, sonipedibus, nemoriuagus.* They invited too the polysyllabic words toward the end of many of my lines, which differ metrically from his in that I have added an unaccented syllable at the end of the line to lighten the second half still further.